Travel Guide To Tenerife 2023

Discover the Enchanting Beauty of Tenerife: Your Ultimate Travel Companion for 2023

Scott O. Cortes

Copyright ©2023,Scott O. Cortes
All rights reserved. No part of this publication may be reproduced, stored in a retrieval system or transmitted in any form or by any means, electronic, mechanical, photocopying, recording or otherwise without prior written permission of the author, expect in the case of brief quotations embodied in critical reviews and certain other noncommercial uses permitted by copyright law.

Table Of Content

INTRODUCTION
- Welcome to Tenerife
- About This Guide
- How to use this Guide
- Practical Information

GETTING STARTED
- Planning Your Trip
- When to Visit Season
- Transportation Options
- Visa and Entry Requirements
- Currency and Banking
- Language and Communication

EXPLORING TENERIFE
- Overview of Tenerife
- Popular Regions and Cities
- Must-Visit Attractions
- Beaches and Coastal Delights
- Natural Wonders and

Landscapes
Cultural and Historical Sites
Outdoor Adventures and Activities

WHERE TO STAY

Tenerife's Accommodation Options
Luxury Resorts and Hotels
Budget Friendly Hotels and Hostels
Charming Bed and Breakfast
Vacation Rentals and Apartments
Camping and Caravan Sites
Unique Accommodations

TASTES OF TENERIFE

Tenerife's Culinary Scene
Traditional Canarian Cuisine
Popular Local Dishes and Specialties

Seafood and Fresh Delights
Dining Experiences and Restaurants
Vegetarian and Vegan Options
Canarian Wines and Beverages

OUTDOOR ADVENTURES

Hiking and Trekking Routes
Scenic Nature Walks
Cycling and Mountain Biking Trails
Water Sports and Activities
Whale and Dolphin Watching
Golfing in Tenerife
Paragliding and Skydiving

SHOPPING AND NIGHTLIFE

Shopping in Tenerife
Local Markets and Souvenirs
Shopping Centers and Mall
Nightlife and Entertainment
Festivals and Events

Performance Arts and Theatres
Casinos and Nightclubs

PRACTICAL TIPS AND SAFETY
Health and Safety Information
Emergency Contacts
Local Customs and Etiquette
Tipping and Bargaining
Transportation Tips
Packing Essential
Travel Insurance
Essential Useful Phrases

DAY TRIPS AND EXCURSIONS
Nearby Islands and Attractions
La Gomera
Mount Teide National Park
Los Gigantes Cliffs
Anaga Rural Park
La Orotava
Garachico And Icod de los Vinos

ITINERARIES AND TRAVEL PLANS

- **One Week in Tenerife**
- **Two Weeks in Tenerife**
- **Family-Friendly Itinerary**
- **Adventure Seeker's Itinerary**
- **Tenerife on a Budget**

CONCLUSION

INTRODUCTION

Welcome to Tenerife

Welcome to Tenerife, a mesmerising location rich in fascinating beauty and unforgettable adventures. Tenerife, located in the centre of the Canary Islands, offers breathtaking scenery, a dynamic culture, and countless options for adventure.

This travel guide will be your best travel companion in 2023 while you explore Tenerife, whether you're looking for sandy beaches, exhilarating outdoor pursuits, or a taste of delectable Canarian food.

You can use the information on these pages to plan your trip and make the most of it. This book is intended to improve your experience in Tenerife by providing useful advice on travel and lodging as well as in-depth explanations of must-see sights and undiscovered gems. Explore charming seaside towns, stroll across stunning volcanic landscapes, become immersed in the island's history and culture, and savour mouthwatering regional specialties.

Discover Tenerife's hidden gems using our suggested itineraries, which have been crafted to fit a variety of interests and travel needs. There is an itinerary that will make your trip special, whether you have a week, two weeks, or are travelling with family. Visit the famous Mount Teide National Park, take day trips to nearby islands, marvel at spectacular natural beauties, and take in the lively atmosphere of Tenerife's festivals and festivities.

You may easily tour the island with the help of useful information, safety advice, and a reference to the local customs, ensuring a smooth and pleasurable journey. You'll get all the resources you need to make priceless memories in Tenerife with suggestions for dining, shopping, and entertainment.

Prepare to go out on a remarkable voyage as you immerse yourself in Tenerife's treasures. In 2023, let this travel manual serve as your entryway to a magical island adventure. Greetings from Tenerife!

About This Guide

Your best travel companion for discovering the allure of Tenerife in 2023 is the book "Travel Guide to Tenerife 2023: Discover the Enchanting Beauty of Tenerife". This detailed and current guide has been painstakingly created to help you get the most out of your trip to this breathtaking location.

What to anticipate from this guide is as follows:

- Information in Detail: The best areas, cities, tourist sites, and natural wonders of Tenerife are all covered in detail in this guide. You'll find practical advice, historical insights, and insider knowledge to help you explore the island and unearth its undiscovered treasures.

- Practical guidance: This guide offers helpful guidance to guarantee a pleasant and trouble-free vacation to Tenerife, covering everything from visa needs to transit alternatives, money and banking, language and communication guidelines, and other crucial elements.

- Recommendations for Lodging and Dining: Find a variety of lodging choices to meet various interests and budgets, including luxury resorts, affordable hotels, beautiful bed and breakfasts, vacation rentals, and more.

  Explore the island's culinary scene as well, with suggestions for authentic Canarian fare, well-known regional delicacies, delicious seafood, and dining establishments that accommodate different dietary restrictions.

- Outdoor Adventures and Activities: This guide offers a wide range of outdoor adventures and activities to satisfy any taste, whether you're a nature lover, a thrill seeker, or just trying to unwind. You'll find ideas for an active and rewarding holiday, including hiking and trekking routes, water activities, wildlife encounters, and golfing.

- Find out where to go shopping, where to go for amusement, where to go for events, and where to go for entertainment when visiting Tenerife. This guide makes sure you don't miss out on the island's rich social scene, which includes both cultural performances and vibrant nightlife.

- Itineraries and Travel Plans: This guide offers suggested itineraries for various lengths of time and interests to help you make the most of your stay on the island. You'll find helpful suggestions to help you plan your trip, whether you choose a family-friendly schedule, an adventure-filled tour, or a relaxation-focused getaway.

- Keep educated and ready with this useful safety and health advice, emergency contacts, local customs, travel ideas, packing basics, and information on the value of travel insurance.

With the help of this in-depth travel guide, get ready to discover Tenerife's entrancing beauty. As you set out on an exciting adventure to one of Spain's most alluring islands, let it be your dependable travel buddy.

How to use this Guide

Here are some suggestions on how to use the "Travel Guide to Tenerife 2023: Discover the Enchanting Beauty of Tenerife" to its fullest potential:

- Get to know yourself: Read the introduction first, which gives you a general idea of what to expect in the guide. Note the topics addressed and the organisation of the guide in the table of contents.

- Plan your trip: If you haven't done so previously, decide how long you'll be in Tenerife and which locations or sites you'd like to visit. You can select the itinerary that best meets your needs from those provided in this guide, which caters to various travel inclinations.

- How to Read the Chapters: Tenerife travel is covered in detail in each chapter. Start with the chapter that most closely relates to your interests or pressing needs as you browse the other chapters. However, don't be afraid to look at other chapters as well, since they can have useful advice in them.

- Go the Descriptions and Tips: As you go through each chapter, take your time to read the in-depth descriptions of the places, things to do, things to see, places to stay, places to eat, and other things. Pay close attention to the useful advice offered, such as information on transportation, the ideal times to visit particular locations, and regional customs to be mindful of.

- Use the Recommendations: This book advises on a variety of travel-related topics, including lodging, food, outdoor activities, shopping, and entertainment. Utilise these tips to make the most of your trip and experience the best that Tenerife has to offer.

- Important Information: You'll find useful details, safety advice, and contact information throughout the guide. Make a note of crucial details including emergency contacts, visa restrictions, travel choices, and regional traditions. This will assist you in being organised and knowledgeable while travelling.

- Customise Your Experience: Although this guide has a plethora of information, feel free to adjust it to suit your tastes. To make your trip special and unforgettable, start with suggestions and then add your discoveries and interests.

- Make use of the Appendix: Don't forget to look at the appendix, which includes helpful resources like a list of words and phrases, suggested reading, maps, and an index. These extra resources can improve your knowledge of and exploration of Tenerife.

The true experience is on the island; keep in mind that this guide is only there to help and inspire you. Explore your surroundings, meet people from the area, and enjoy Tenerife's allure. Have fun on your trip!

Practical Information

To guarantee a smooth and pleasurable journey, it's crucial to have useful information at your fingertips while making travel plans to Tenerife. The following are some crucial, realistic considerations:

- Before departing for Tenerife, be sure to check the visa requirements for your country of residence. Depending on your nationality, you could be able to enter without a visa or you might need to apply for a visa ahead of time. Make sure your passport is still valid for the entire time you will be there.

- The Euro (€) is the official unit of exchange in Tenerife and the rest of Spain. It is recommended to exchange some money before your travel or to use an ATM to get Euros after you arrive. On the island, ATMs are widely dispersed, and most businesses take credit cards.

- Spanish is the language of the government in Tenerife. However, English is extensively spoken at hotels, eateries, and tourist areas as a result of the island's prominence as a vacation spot. It can be useful to know a few fundamental Spanish words and phrases, particularly when communicating with people in less visited places.

- Check with your mobile service provider about the availability of international roaming to stay in touch while travelling. As an alternative, you can buy a local SIM card for your unlocked smartphone when you are there. Additionally, free Wi-Fi is frequently accessible in hotels, cafes, and public spaces.

- Tenerife generally maintains high standards for healthcare and cleanliness. It is advised to obtain travel insurance that includes emergency evacuation and coverage for medical costs. Learn how to reach medical facilities and emergency services, including by dialling 112 for a universal emergency.

- Western European Time (WET) and Western European Summer Time (WEST) are the two time zones in use in Tenerife, respectively. Tenerife shares the same time zone (GMT+0/GMT+1) as the United Kingdom.

- Transportation: The transportation system in Tenerife is highly developed. There are frequent flights from significant European cities to the island's two main airports, Tenerife North Airport (TFN) and Tenerife South Airport (TFS). Buses, taxis, and rented cars are all considered public transportation. Tenerife can be reached by ferry from other Canary Islands as well.

- Tenerife has a mild, pleasant environment all year long, making it a well-liked vacation spot for sun worshippers. Pack comfortable walking shoes and lightweight, breathable clothing. Additionally, it's a good idea to pack sunglasses, a hat, and sunscreen to protect yourself from the sun.

- Electrical Outlets: The usual plug type in Tenerife is the European two-pin plug (Type C/F), and the electrical voltage ranges from 220-240V. You might want a travel adaptor if the plugs on your gadgets are different.

- Tenerife has its own set of customs and etiquette, just like the rest of Spain. It's customary to give someone a handshake or a cheek kiss when you first meet them. Tipping is generally done by rounding up the check or adding 10%; however, it is not required. When visiting holy sites, dress modestly and respect regional traditions and customs.

You can make sure that your trip to Tenerife is smooth and well-planned by keeping these practical considerations in mind. Enjoy your journey and take in all the island has to offer!

GETTING STARTED

Planning Your Trip

A successful and pleasurable trip to Tenerife depends on preparation. When planning your trip, take the following factors into account:

- **Best Time to Visit:** Tenerife is a wonderful location all year round due to its moderate climate. However, the summer months (June to August) are when the island experiences its heaviest visitor traffic. If you want nice weather and less visitors, go in the shoulder seasons (spring and autumn).

- Decide how long you'll be in Tenerife before you arrive. The number of activities and sites you can include into your agenda depends on how long it is. Make sure you set aside enough time, whether you have a few days or a few weeks, to explore the various areas and take advantage of the island's many attractions.

- **Interests and Preferences**: When creating your itinerary, take into account your interests and preferences. Tenerife provides a variety of activities, including beach relaxation, gastronomic delights, cultural encounters, and outdoor excursions. Prioritise those elements of the island that you find most appealing in your plan.

- Make a list of the attractions you absolutely must see by researching the must-see attractions in Tenerife. This may include well-known sites like the Pyramids of Guimar, La Orotava, Masca

Valley, Mount Teide, and the Teide National Park. Include these places on your agenda, giving yourself plenty of time to explore and take in their beauty.

- Tenerife is a place with a vibrant native culture and traditions. Think about integrating immersion activities in your itinerary, such as going to local markets, taking part in local festivals and events, eating local cuisine, and interacting with the locals. These encounters will help people connect with the island and understand it better.

- **Outdoor Recreation**: Tenerife is a haven for nature lovers. Plan time in your schedule for excursions like hiking, snorkelling, surfing, or cycling if you prefer to do these things. Plan your trip to take advantage of the island's natural beauty by researching the best beaches, water sports venues, and popular routes.

- **Excursions & day trips**: Tenerife is conveniently located for excursions to nearby islands and tourist hotspots. Places like La Gomera, Loro Parque, Los Gigantes Cliffs, or the Anaga Rural Park are worth adding as additional excursions. These day tours will broaden your understanding of the Canary Islands' diversity, which will improve your experience on Tenerife.

- While exploring the island is fun, don't forget to schedule some downtime for unwinding. Tenerife has lovely beaches, serene spa resorts, and scenic locations where you may relax and rejuvenate. Include relaxed times to take in the island's natural beauty and atmosphere to balance out your schedule.

- Take into account factors that are realistic, such as finances, lodging, and transportation. If you're thinking about renting a car, taking the bus, or using a combination of the two, do your research first.

  Investigate several lodging options, such as hotels, resorts, vacation rentals, or neighbourhood guesthouses, to determine which one best suits your requirements and price range.

- **Flexibility**: While having a well-planned itinerary is important, you should also allow for some latitude while travelling. Allow time for unforeseen discoveries, impromptu side trips, and local advice. When you accept the unexpected and follow the flow, the most remarkable moments frequently occur.

You may design a well-rounded and memorable itinerary for your vacation to Tenerife by taking these elements into account and personalising it to your tastes. Enjoy the planning process and be ready for an amazing vacation on this wonderful island!

When to Visit Season

With a lovely climate all year long, Tenerife provides guests with a unique experience no matter the season. Your preferences and interests might, however, be better served by particular seasons of the year than by others. When choosing a date to visit Tenerife, keep the following things in mind:

- **Weather**: Because of its location off the northwest coast of Africa, Tenerife experiences warm winters and spring-like summers. It is a desirable location all year round because the average temperature ranges from 20°C (68°F) in the winter to 28°C (82°F) in the summer.

    The summer months (June to August) provide the highest temperatures if you want longer, sunnier days. Autumn (September to November) and spring (March to May) offer excellent weather and less tourists.

- **Crowds and Peak Season:** Tenerife is often busiest throughout the summer (June to August) and around Christmas and New Year, when a greater number of visitors arrive.

Consider going in the shoulder seasons of spring and autumn if you want a more relaxing experience and to avoid crowds. You may explore the island at a more leisurely pace during these months thanks to a balance of nice weather and less visitors.

- Tenerife offers a number of festivals and events all through the year to highlight its rich culture and customs. Plan your visit appropriately if you want to take part in these lively celebrations.

One of the most renowned and magnificent events on the island is the Carnival of Santa Cruz de Tenerife, which takes place in February or March. The Corpus Christi celebrations in June and the San Andrés festival in November are two further noteworthy festivals.

- **Outdoor Activities:** The varied topography of Tenerife offers a wealth of options for outdoor pursuits like hiking, sea sports, and discovering the island's natural marvels.

Think on the exact activities you want to do and research the best times of year to do them. For instance, spring and autumn offer pleasant weather for outdoor experiences whether you want to walk in the mountains or explore the Teide National Park.

- **Observing wildlife:** Dolphins and whales are among the diverse marine species found in abundance in Tenerife. You can see these animals all year long if you're interested in wildlife viewing.

Weather and ocean temperatures can, however, change. While the winter months may present an opportunity to observe certain species' migration, the summer months typically offer calmer seas, making it easier to spot marine life.

- **Budget**: Take into account the price of travel and lodging throughout various seasons. During periods of strong travel demand, such as the summer and significant holidays, airfares and hotel rates may increase. Consider going during the shoulder seasons or low season if you're travelling on a budget to take advantage of potential discounts and deals.

The best time to travel to Tenerife ultimately comes down to your own preferences, desired activities, and availability. Tenerife offers a warm experience all year long, whether you prefer peaceful exploration, cultural festivals, or hot summer days.

Transportation Options

Tenerife has a selection of modes of transportation to make it easy for you to go around and enjoy the island. The primary forms of transportation are as follows:

- **Car rental:** For those who prefer the freedom to explore Tenerife at their own leisure, renting a car is a popular option. There are numerous automobile rental agencies on the island, and you may book one at the airport or in popular tourist regions and large towns.

    You can get to more distant places, picturesque vistas, and off-the-beaten-path things if you have a car. Remember that in Tenerife, driving is done on the right side of the road.

- **Public Buses**: TITSA (Transportes Interurbanos de Tenerife) manages a sizable network of public buses in Tenerife. Bus routes cover the major cities, tourism hotspots, and attractions.

  The buses run on a regular schedule and are reasonably priced. Santa Cruz de Tenerife and Puerto de la Cruz are home to the primary bus stations. Tickets can be bought at specific kiosks or onboard the ship.

- **Taxis**: In all sections of Tenerife, notably in tourist hubs, cities, and airports, taxis are easily accessible. The fares for taxis are controlled, and they run on a metered system. It is advised to make sure the driver starts the metre at the start of the journey. Taxis can be located at designated taxi stops or hailed on the street. It's a practical choice for shorter trips or while hauling luggage.

- **Trams**: Tranvia de Tenerife is the name of the tram system in Tenerife. The Santa Cruz de Tenerife and La Laguna metropolitan areas are served by the tram. It is a cutting-edge and effective means of transportation, especially for navigating city centres. The tram connects a number of attractions and is a great way to avoid traffic and parking issues.

- Ferries are an option if you want to visit other Canary Islands or go on day trips to neighbouring islands. Between Tenerife and islands like Gran Canaria, La Gomera, and La Palma, there are frequent ferry connections. Santa Cruz de Tenerife and Los

Cristianos are the locations of the island's two primary ferry ports.

- **Excursions and Tours:** There are many tour companies that provide escorted excursions and tours of Tenerife. If you prefer organised transportation and wish to see particular places or partake in particular activities, these can be a practical option. Transportation, a tour guide, and attraction admission costs are all possible components of excursions.

- Bicycles and scooters are available for rent in Tenerife, especially in popular spots and along the coast. The best way to explore bike paths, seaside roads, and oceanfront promenades is with this method of transportation. It offers a more leisurely and environmentally responsible method to explore the island.

Take into account your own tastes, the duration of your trip, and the exact destinations you intend to visit when selecting your mode of transportation.

It is advised to verify availability, prices, and timetables in advance, especially during the busiest travel times. Tenerife offers a variety of transportation choices, making it simple for you to go around and enjoy your vacation.

Visa and Entry Requirements

It's crucial to be aware of the entry and visa procedures specific to your country while organising your trip to Tenerife. For your reference, the following general information:

- **Citizens of Member States of the European Union (EU):** If you are a citizen of an EU member state, you do not require a visa to enter Spain or Tenerife. A valid passport or national identity card entitles you to unrestricted travel.

- **Citizens of the Schengen Area**: Tenerife is a part of the Schengen Area, which is made up of many non-EU nations as well as the majority of EU members. Without a visa, citizens of Schengen Area nations may travel to Tenerife and remain there for up to 90 days during a 180-day span. Make sure your passport is valid for at least six months after the day you intend to depart.

- **Non-EU Nationals**: If you are a national of a nation that is not a member of the EU or the Schengen Zone, you might need a visa to enter Tenerife. Your country of citizenship determines the precise visa requirements. The Spanish embassy or consulate in your country, or the appropriate authorities, should be contacted to find out the visa requirements, application procedure, and paperwork needed for your visit.

- **Visa-Free Travel**: Spain has visa waiver agreements with a number of nations, enabling their nationals to visit or conduct business in Tenerife for a brief period of time without obtaining a visa. The amount of time that can be spent there varies per nation. Upon arrival, citizens of these nations usually acquire a stamp that entitles them to a stay in Tenerife for up to 90 days within a 180-day window. Make sure your passport is current and has at least six months left on it.

- You must apply for a visa at the Spanish embassy or consulate in your home country if you need one to enter Tenerife. A completed visa application form, a current passport, recent photos, proof of travel insurance, proof of lodging, financial records, and an itinerary in detail may all be required as part of the application process.

Since processing timelines for visas can vary, it is best to apply well in advance of your intended travel dates.

- **Travel insurance**: Having travel insurance that covers medical costs, trip cancellation or interruption, and emergency medical evacuation is strongly advised, however it is not required for all visitors. Verify that any specific activities or sports you intend to participate in are covered by your insurance policy, and that it is valid for the entire time of your visit to Tenerife.

It's crucial to keep in mind that visa and entry requirements can alter, so it's advisable to confirm the most recent details with the relevant authorities or diplomatic missions well in advance of your trip. Based on your nationality and unique situation, they can give you the most precise and recent information.

You can guarantee a simple and trouble-free trip to this lovely island resort by being aware of the Tenerife visa and entry requirements.

Currency and Banking

The Euro (€) is the official currency of Tenerife and the rest of Spain. Here is some information about banking services and currency exchange in Tenerife:

- **Currency Exchange**: Banks, exchange offices, and a few hotels in Tenerife are places where you may exchange your foreign currency for Euros. Banks normally provide cheap exchange rates but can have sporadic hours of operation.

    Additionally prevalent in tourist locations are exchange offices, or "cambios," which provide practical exchange services. Before engaging in a purchase, it is a good idea to examine exchange rates and costs.

- **Automated Teller Machines (ATMs)** are widely available in Tenerife and accept most popular debit and credit cards from across the world. Banks, retail establishments, and tourist destinations all have ATMs.

To guarantee that your card will function overseas, be sure to let your bank or card issuer know about your travel intentions. Remember that some ATMs may charge a fee for withdrawals, and it's best to withdraw more money to save transaction expenses.

- **Credit Cards:** In Tenerife, especially for hotels, restaurants, bigger stores, and tourist attractions, credit cards—particularly Visa and Mastercard—are widely accepted. Smaller stores, markets, and neighbourhood businesses might favour cash transactions. Always keep some cash on hand as a safety net, especially for smaller purchases or while travelling to distant locations where card acceptance can be spotty.

- The regular banking hours in Tenerife are Monday through Friday, with shortened hours on Saturdays and closed on Sundays. The typical opening hours are from 9:00 AM to 2:00 PM, while certain banks may maintain later hours in busy towns or popular tourist destinations. ATMs are open around-the-clock for simple transactions including cash withdrawals.

- Traveler's checks are no longer as readily recognized as they once were. In Tenerife, it could be difficult to find places that welcome them. As a result, it's wise to rely on other payment methods, such cash or credit cards.

- **Safety and Precautions**: It's important to take precautions to guarantee your safety when using ATMs or carrying cash. Protect the keypad when entering your PIN and only use ATMs that are situated in well-lit, secure areas. To avoid theft or pickpocketing, keep a watch on your valuables, particularly in crowded situations.

- **Currency Exchange Advice**: To obtain the greatest value, compare exchange rates before exchanging money. Avoid doing your currency exchange at airports or in popular tourist regions because the prices there are frequently worse. To reduce transaction costs, take into account transferring greater sums all at once.

- To avoid any potential problems with card usage, it's always a good idea to let your bank or credit card provider know about your vacation plans. In case of any issues or lost cards, it's also advised to retain a list of the emergency phone numbers for your bank and card issuers.

You can make sure that your financial activities go smoothly and that you have easy access to money while visiting Tenerife by being knowledgeable about the currency exchange choices and banking services available there.

Language and Communication

The majority of Spain, including Tenerife, speaks Spanish as its native language. The following details pertain to language and communication in Tenerife:

- The official language of Tenerife is Spanish, primarily the Castilian dialect. Spanish is the primary language of the vast majority of the local populace. Knowing a few fundamental Spanish words and phrases might be useful when visiting Tenerife, especially when interacting with people who might not speak perfect English.

- **English Proficiency**: You can typically find people who speak English in well-known tourist destinations and larger cities, like Santa Cruz de Tenerife and Playa de las Américas. Locals' levels of English proficiency may vary, with younger generations and those employed in the tourism sector frequently having a stronger grasp of the language. However, English proficiency may be limited in more rural or less visited areas. Having a pocket phrasebook or language translation app on you is always a good idea.

- There are several tourist information centres in Tenerife where you can get assistance and information in English. These locations, which offer maps, brochures, and information on activities, attractions, and transportation, are in popular tourist areas.

- **Menus and Signage**: You can frequently find menus and signage in English as well as other languages in well-known tourist destinations and eateries that welcome foreign tourists. However, menus may be primarily in Spanish in smaller neighbourhood restaurants. Understanding common Spanish food terminology can make it easier for you to navigate menus.

- **Tools and Language Apps:** If you don't speak Spanish well, using tools and/or language translation apps can help you communicate. To make it simpler to communicate with locals, these apps can help you translate words, phrases, and even real-time conversation translations.

- **Cultural etiquette and politeness:** Depending on the time of day, it is polite to say "Buenos dias" (Good morning), "Buenas tardes" (Good afternoon), or "Buenas noches" (Good evening/night) when interacting with locals. Basic greetings and expressions in Spanish, like "Por favour" (Please) and "Gracias" (Thank you), can help build rapport and demonstrate respect.

- **Multicultural Destination with Diverse Community:** Tenerife is home to a diverse community. In addition to Spanish, you might hear people speaking English, German, French, and Italian, especially in touristy areas and hotels.

- Keep in mind that trying your best to communicate in the local tongue, even with simple phrases, can enrich your cultural experience. Don't be afraid to ask for assistance or clarification if necessary; locals are typically welcoming and understanding of tourists.

You can navigate communication during your trip to Tenerife and forge lasting relationships with the locals by being aware of language dynamics and using language tools.

EXPLORING TENERIFE

Overview of Tenerife

The Canary Islands, an archipelago in the Atlantic Ocean that is a part of Spain, with Tenerife as its largest and most populous island. Tenerife draws millions of tourists each year thanks to its breathtaking natural scenery, lively culture, and moderate weather all year round.
Here is a description of this beautiful island:

- Geographically, Tenerife is an island off the coast of northwest Africa that was formed by volcanic activity. The majestic Mount Teide, a dormant volcano and the highest point in Spain towers over the island. The scenery is varied, with parched plains and breathtaking coastline cliffs in the south contrasted with lush valleys and forests in the north.

- **Climate**: Tenerife has a subtropical climate with comfortable weather all year round. Average temperatures on the island range from 20°C (68°F) in winter to 30°C (86°F) in summer, with warm summers and mild winters. Tenerife's north is typically more humid and lush, whereas its south is typically sunnier and dryer.

- Tenerife has a diverse cultural legacy that is impacted by its Guanche native roots, Spanish customs, and outside influences. The island holds a variety of vibrant festivals and events all year long that feature local cuisine, dance, and music. The cuisine of Tenerife is varied, with regional delicacies such as local pastries, mojo sauces, fresh seafood, and Canarian potatoes (papas arrugadas).

- Tenerife is a well-liked vacation spot with a variety of sights and activities. Beautiful sandy and volcanic beaches on the island are ideal for relaxing, swimming, and participating in water sports. Adventure sports like paragliding and surfing are available for outdoor enthusiasts, as well as hiking paths and whale viewing.

   It is essential to explore the Teide National Park, which features stunning volcanic scenery and is a UNESCO World Heritage Site.

- **Cities and Towns:** Santa Cruz de Tenerife, the capital city of Tenerife, is a bustling cosmopolitan centre with a combination of modern and old architecture, shopping areas, and a boisterous carnival celebration. Other significant towns are Costa Adeje, a famous tourist destination with five-star hotels, golf courses, and entertainment options, and Puerto de la Cruz, famed for its picturesque old town and botanical gardens.

- **Travel**: Tenerife boasts an efficient transportation system that makes it simple to tour the island. There are transportation options including taxis, public buses, and rental automobiles.

  Additionally, the cities of Santa Cruz de Tenerife and La Laguna have tram services. Ferry services also link Tenerife to the other Canary Islands.

Tenerife provides a wide variety of experiences, from tranquil beach vacations to exhilarating outdoor pursuits. It is an alluring place for tourists looking for an unforgettable vacation because of its natural beauty, mild environment, and active culture.

Popular Regions and Cities

Tenerife is a varied island with various distinctive areas and cities that provide visitors with one-of-a-kind experiences. Here are some of the well-liked areas and cities to visit:

- **Santa Cruz de Tenerife** is the capital of Tenerife and is a bustling, international city. It is situated on the island's northeastern shore. It is renowned for its vibrant carnival celebrations, contemporary architecture, commercial areas like Calle Castillo, and cultural landmarks like the famed concert theatre Auditorio de Tenerife.

- **Puerto de la Cruz** is a wonderful town with a fascinating history and a beautiful old town. It is located on the northern coast. It is also known for its stunning black sand beaches, the botanical gardens, the elegant Casa de la Aduana, and the lush and well-kept Lago Martianez pool complex.

- A well-liked vacation destination, Costa Adeje is noted for its opulent hotels, gorgeous beaches, and luxury amenities. It is situated on the country's southwest coast. It provides a variety of water sports activities, such as scuba diving, sailing, and jet skiing. Additionally, visitors can take pleasure in shopping at Plaza del Duque and visit the well-known water park, Siam Park.

- **Los Cristianos**: A former fishing community that has evolved into a thriving tourist destination, Los Cristianos is located on the southern coast. It has lovely sandy beaches, a charming harbour, and a bustling promenade surrounded by eateries, bars, and stores. You can take a ferry from the harbour to other Canary Islands.

- **La Laguna:** La Laguna, a historic village and UNESCO World Heritage Site, is situated inland. Before Santa Cruz de Tenerife, it served as the island's capital. Grand houses and churches, as well as well-preserved colonial architecture, can be seen at La Laguna. One of the oldest universities in the Canary Islands, the University of La Laguna, is also located in the town.

- **El Teide National Park**: The Teide National Park, located in the middle of the island, is a must-see destination. With beautiful volcanic scenery, hiking trails of varied difficulty, and expansive vistas of the island, it includes

Mount Teide, the highest mountain in Spain. Visitors can reach the summit on a cable car for breathtaking views.

- Anaga Rural Park is a haven for nature lovers and is situated in the northeastern region of the island. It has majestic mountains, old laurel forests, and charming coastal settlements. With clearly marked paths leading to vistas, isolated beaches, and beautiful hamlets, the park provides excellent hiking options.

These sites and cities in Tenerife provide a variety of experiences, from cultural immersion in old towns to beach relaxation in well-known tourist destinations. Every location on this alluring island has its allure and attractions, guaranteeing that there is something to interest every tourist.

Must-Visit Attractions

Visitors can experience a variety of activities on the alluring island of Tenerife. Following are some of Tenerife's must-see attractions, which range from gorgeous natural scenery to cultural treasures:

- **Teide National Park** is one of Tenerife's most well-known attractions and is situated in the island's centre. Teide National Park is a UNESCO World Heritage Site. Mount Teide, a dormant volcano and Spain's tallest mountain dominates the park. The park's pathways, unusual rock formations, and surreal vistas may all be explored after taking a cable car ride to the top for stunning views of the volcanic landscapes.

- **Masca Village** is recognized for its breathtaking natural surroundings and is located in the

Teno Mountains to the northwest of Tenerife. This charming settlement offers breathtaking views of deep ravines and verdant landscapes and is encircled by towering cliffs. For a memorable journey, wander through the winding alleyways, go to the lovely church, and trek through the Masca Gorge.

- **Loro Parque** is a renowned animal and theme park that is a must-see for families and animal enthusiasts. It is situated in Puerto de la Cruz. The park features exciting shows, instructive exhibitions, and exquisitely designed gardens. It is home to a variety of species, including dolphins, killer whales, penguins, and exotic birds.

- **Siam Park:** One of the best water parks in the world is located in

Costa Adeje. The park offers exhilarating water slides, a lazy river, a wave pool, and a sandy beach that are all inspired by Thai architecture and culture. Take pleasure in thrilling attractions like the Tower of Power or unwind in the tropical setting.

- **Anaga Rural Park**: The northeastern region of the island is home to Anaga Rural Park, a haven for those who love the outdoors. Ancient laurel trees, rough mountains, and breathtaking coastline views can all be found in this protected natural region. Discover the network of hiking routes that take you past beautiful scenery, hidden beaches, and lush forests.

- Visit the lovely town of Garachico on Tenerife's northwest coast. Beautiful buildings, cobblestone streets, and a lovely harbour are all features of this mediaeval town. Visit the old San Miguel Castle, take a stroll around the town's attractive squares and gardens, and explore the natural rock pools known as El Caletón.

- **Pyramids of Gümar**: Explore the mysterious Pyramids of Gümar, which are situated in the Gümar Valley on Tenerife's east coast. The indigenous Guanche people are thought to have constructed these six-step lava stone pyramids. Discover the mystery of the pyramids, stroll through the lovely botanical gardens, and explore the Ethnographic Park.

- **La Orotava:** Discover the lovely streets and well-preserved traditional architecture of this historic town. Visit Casa de los

Balcones, a stunning mansion from the 17th century that displays classic Canarian design, and stroll through the town's historic district to see the spectacular mansions, ornate churches, and peaceful plazas.

These are just a few of Tenerife's numerous must-see attractions. Tenerife provides a wide variety of unique sites and activities that suit all travellers' interests, whether you're looking for natural beauty, cultural encounters, or family-friendly fun.

Beaches and Coastal Delights

Tenerife is well known for its beautiful beaches and scenic coastlines. The island provides a multitude of coastal attractions thanks to its varied shoreline, which spans from pristine golden sand beaches to towering volcanic cliffs. Some of Tenerife's must-see beaches and coastal locations are included below:

- One of the most famous and stunning beaches on the island is Playa de las Teresitas, which is close to Santa Cruz de Tenerife. This 1.5-kilometer stretch of golden sand beach is bordered by palm palms. The beach has facilities including sun loungers and beach bars, and the calm seas are ideal for swimming.

- **Playa de la Tejita**: Playa de la Tejita is a calm, undeveloped beach that is found in the southern part of Tenerife, close to El Médano. The strong winds and clean waters of this expansive sandy beach, which is backed by a picturesque red mountain, make it a favourite destination for windsurfers and kiteboarders.

- On Tenerife's western coast is a place called Los Gigantes, which is well-known for its towering cliffs that plunge sharply into the water. The region provides boat trips to see the cliffs up close and breath-taking views. Small, isolated coves can be found close by where you can unwind and take in the natural beauty of the rocky shoreline.

- **El Médano** is a well-known beach hamlet in the southeast of the island that is well-known for its windsurfing and kitesurfing conditions. While the town itself offers a laid-back vibe with its picturesque promenade, beachside cafes, and restaurants, the long sandy beach is ideal for water sport aficionados.

- **Playa de Benijo:** Playa de Benijo, a gorgeous black sand beach encircled by towering cliffs, is located in the Anaga Rural Park on the northeastern coast. It's renowned for its untamed beauty that's rough and unrefined, providing a sense of seclusion and tranquillity. For those looking for a more untouched and natural coastal experience, the beach is perfect.

- **Playa Jardin:** Playa Jardin, a gorgeously designed beach built by renowned artist César Manrique, is situated in Puerto de la Cruz. It has rich gardens, black volcanic sand, and unusual architectural characteristics. There are various portions of the beach, each with its own appeal and services.

- Playa San Juan is a calm, good for families beach that is located in the southwest of Tenerife. There are calm waves, a large stretch of golden sand, and a boardwalk lined with eateries. Spend a lazy day at the beach or wander along the promenade to take in the breathtaking coastline views.

- **Punta de Teno:** Punta de Teno, on the northwest coast of Tenerife, is a wild and lonely coastal region renowned for its towering cliffs and untamable beauty. The region offers breath-taking views of the Atlantic Ocean and is reachable via a beautiful road. Please be aware that due to preservation activities, access to Punta de Teno may occasionally be limited.

These are only a few of Tenerife's breathtaking beaches and coastal attractions. Tenerife's many coastal regions offer a variety of possibilities to suit every preference, whether you're seeking for sunbathing, water activities, or simply to take in the natural beauty of the shoreline.

Natural Wonders and Landscapes

Tenerife is blessed with a wide variety of beautiful natural features and vistas. The island offers a wide variety of natural attractions, including imposing volcanic peaks, luxuriant forests, and beautiful coasts. Here are some of Tenerife's top natural landmarks and settings:

- The stunning and recognizable natural wonder known as Mount Teide is the highest peak in Spain. The UNESCO-listed Teide National Park encircles this inactive volcano, which is 3,718 metres (12,198 ft) tall. Visit the park's footpaths, lava fields, and unusual rock formations, or take a cable car ride to the park's summit for panoramic views of the island.

- **Masca Gorge**: This natural wonder, which is situated in the island's northwest, provides breathtaking hiking opportunities. Towering cliffs, abundant greenery, and a meandering trail that descends to the seclusion of Masca Beach can all be found in the gorge. Although the trek can be difficult, you'll be rewarded with breathtaking vistas along the way.

- Anaga Rural Park is a haven for nature lovers and is located in the northeastern region of Tenerife. Ancient laurel forests, untamed mountains, and spectacular coastline vistas define this protected region.

Discover secret beaches, explore the network of hiking trails that take you through beautiful woodlands, and take in the peace and quiet of this unspoiled natural setting.

- Los Roques de Garca is a bizarre rock formation that displays the island's volcanic origins. It is found within Teide National Park. These striking rock formations, including the well-known Roque Cinchado, lie in a lunar-like setting and offer tourists a singular and mesmerising spectacle.

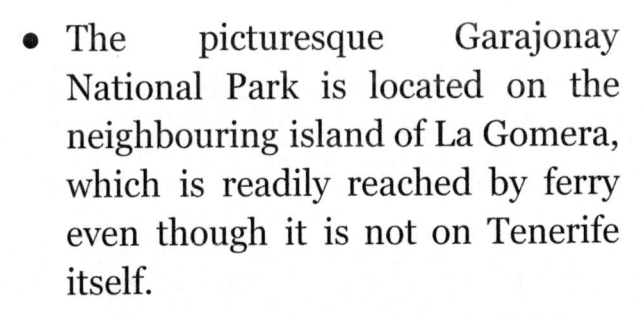

- The picturesque Garajonay National Park is located on the neighbouring island of La Gomera, which is readily reached by ferry even though it is not on Tenerife itself.

  This UNESCO World Heritage Site is home to centuries-old laurel forests, foggy valleys, and sweeping vistas. Explore this nearby island's natural splendour by hiking through its lush woodland pathways.

- **Cliffs of Los Gigantes:** The Cliffs of Los Gigantes are a striking natural landmark that may be found on Tenerife's western shore. These enormous cliffs plunge sharply into the water, rising up to 600 metres (1,970 feet) in height. Take a boat ride along the coast to see these magnificent cliffs in all their majesty.

- **La Orotava Valley:** Located in Tenerife's northern region, the La Orotava Valley is renowned for its breathtaking views. Banana plantations, vineyards with terraces, and lovely villages are scattered throughout this lush valley. Discover La Orotava, a typical town, and its well-preserved architecture and lovely gardens.

- **Teno Rural Park:** The Teno Rural Park is a rough and lonely region with magnificent coastline cliffs, deep ravines, and secret coves. It is situated in the northwest portion of the island. Drive through this natural park's meandering roads, and you'll be rewarded with stunning views of the Atlantic Ocean and the surroundings.

These Tenerife natural attractions and settings highlight the island's amazing geological structures, luxuriant vegetation, and breathtaking views.

Tenerife provides a wealth of unspoiled natural beauty to discover and appreciate, whether you're an outdoor enthusiast, a nature lover, or just looking for peace and quiet in beautiful surroundings.

Cultural and Historical Sites

Tenerife is endowed with both natural beauty and a rich cultural and historical past. The island is home to several historical and cultural landmarks that provide insight into its enthralling past and thriving local culture. Here are some of Tenerife's most important cultural and historic locations:

- **La Laguna Historic Centre:** The La Laguna Historic Centre is a UNESCO World Heritage Site and is a veritable architectural treasure trove. Visit the magnificent La Laguna Cathedral, stroll through the cobblestone lanes dotted with colourful homes, and take in the impressive colonial structures that formerly served as the island's principal commerce hub.

- San Cristóbal de La Laguna is another attractive hamlet with a rich cultural legacy that is close to

La Laguna. Discover the town's history as the previous capital of Tenerife by strolling through the well maintained old centre and stopping by the gorgeous Iglesia de la Concepción.

- The historic palace known as Casa de los Balcones, which is located near La Orotava, is an excellent example of Canarian style architecture. Explore the lovely courtyards, take in the ornate wooden balconies, and discover the island's customs and traditions.

- **Museum of Nature and Man:** The Museum of Nature and Man (Museo de la Naturaleza y el Hombre), which is situated in Santa Cruz de Tenerife, is a remarkable cultural centre that displays the natural history of the island, including its volcanic origins and the native Guanche culture. Learn about the Guanche society, explore the archaeological relics, and get to know Tenerife's distinctive flora and animals.

- Discover the mysterious Pyramids of Gümar, which are situated in the Gümar Valley. These six-step pyramids, which are thought to have been constructed by the local Guanche people, provide a fascinating look into Tenerife's pre-Hispanic past. Discover the wonders of the pyramids and the lovely plant gardens of the Ethnographic Park.

- **The Santa Cruz de Tenerife Auditorium (Auditorio de Tenerife)** is a modern architectural masterpiece and a symbol of the island's culture. Santiago Calatrava created this magnificent concert hall, which features a year-round schedule of performances and cultural events. If you get the chance, take in a performance and admire its unique design.

- **Casa Iriarte** is a historic house-museum in Puerto de la Cruz that offers insights into life on the island in the 18th century. Experience a step back in time as you look around the beautifully preserved chambers and discover Tenerife's past and customs.

- **The Guanche Archaeological Park (Parque Arqueológico Cueva Pintada),** which is situated in the municipality of Arona, provides a window into the way of life of the prehistoric Guanche people. Discover the archaeological site, which has caverns, reconstructed Guanche homes, and rock engravings to learn more about Tenerife's indigenous culture.

Tenerife's cultural and historical attractions give a fascinating look back at the island's past, exhibiting its rich heritage and giving tourists a chance to fully experience it. There is a lot of Tenerife's fascinating cultural tapestry to discover and learn, from historical cities to museums and archaeological parks.

Outdoor Adventures and Activities

Tenerife is a haven for outdoor lovers and those looking for adventure, offering a wide variety of exhilarating activities in its breathtaking natural settings. The island offers a wide range of outdoor pursuits, from hiking and water sports to wildlife encounters. The following are some of the best outdoor pursuits and adventures in Tenerife:

- Trekking through the magnificent Masca Gorge in Tenerife's northwest is an amazing hike that you may take. This is a difficult yet worthwhile excursion because of the rocky terrain, high cliffs, and rich foliage. As you make your way down to the remote Masca Beach, take in the breathtaking scenery.

- **El Médano** is a popular coastal town noted for its winds and waves. While there, you may engage in exhilarating water sports like windsurfing and kitesurfing. Strong winds and ideal weather make it a haven for lovers of water sports.

- Tenerife is a fantastic site for viewing whales and dolphins in their natural habitat. Take a boat excursion from one of the coastal villages, such Los Cristianos or Puerto de la Cruz, and revel in the breathtaking experience of getting up close and personal with these amazing creatures.

- Fly above Tenerife's magnificent scenery with a paragliding trip. Paragliding in Adeje. Adeje, which is situated in the southwest of the island, provides excellent paragliding conditions and gives breathtaking aerial views of the coastline and mountains.

- Snorkelling and diving are two great ways to explore Tenerife's rich underwater world. Explore the crystal-clear waters that are home to an abundance of marine life, vibrant coral reefs, and even underwater volcanic structures. For these activities, the waters of Los Cristianos and Costa Adeje are particularly well-liked.

- Teide National Park Jeep Safari: Set off on an exhilarating Jeep safari tour through the untamed landscape of Teide National Park. Explore volcanic terrain, take in breath-taking views, and discover the park's distinctive flora and animals. The journey offers a distinctive viewpoint of the island's natural attractions.

- Arico is a well-known Tenerife rock climbing site. Try out your climbing prowess there by scaling the rocks. It delivers an adrenaline-pumping experience amidst stunning scenery and offers a variety of climbing routes appropriate for different skill levels.

- Mountain biking in La Esperanza: La Esperanza is a mountainous area in the northeast of Tenerife. Go on a mountain bike trip here. Experience the thrill of riding along the island's picturesque routes as you explore the many scenery, from deep forests to harsh mountains.

- Experience a forest adventure in Anaga Rural Park, where you can take part in sports like zip-lining, tree climbing, and rope courses amidst the breathtaking natural scenery. It's the ideal choice for anyone looking for an adrenaline rush in a gorgeous woodland environment.

- **Teide National Park** is a great place to observe the stars because of the island's beautiful skies and minimal light pollution. A professional astronomer will lead you on a stargazing trip in Teide National Park where you can admire the grandeur of the night sky while learning about the constellations and other celestial objects.

Tenerife's outdoor pursuits and adventures offer fascinating encounters and chances to interact with the island's natural beauties. Tenerife has much to offer every outdoor enthusiast, whether they prefer quiet exploration or heart-pounding adventures.

WHERE TO STAY

Tenerife's Accommodation Options

Tenerife provides a variety of lodging choices to meet the requirements and tastes of every visitor. You can choose from a wide range of accommodations on the island, including opulent resorts, affordable motels, and comfortable vacation homes.

Here are a few of the most well-liked lodging choices in Tenerife:

- Tenerife is home to a large number of resorts and hotels, especially in well-known tourist destinations like Costa Adeje, Playa de las Américas, and Puerto de la Cruz. These lodging options range from opulent 5-star resorts with all-inclusive features to cosy mid-range motels with a wide range of amenities.

- **Boutique Hotels**: Think about staying at one of Tenerife's boutique hotels if you want a more exclusive and distinctive experience. These more intimate lodgings frequently include chic furnishings, attentive service, and a charming atmosphere. Boutique hotels can be located both inland and in coastal communities.

- Apartments, villas, and holiday houses are just a few of the vacation rentals available in Tenerife. This choice offers versatility, seclusion, and the chance to enjoy the island in a "home away from home" setting. There are a variety of vacation rentals available, accommodating different party sizes and price ranges.

- **Rural Houses**: Tenerife's interior, especially the northern region of the island, provides the opportunity to stay in traditional rural homes known as "casas rurales." Often surrounded by stunning scenery and offering a tranquil getaway away from the busy tourist regions, these lodgings offer a rustic and genuine experience.

- **Bed and Breakfasts**: Tenerife has some charming inns, especially in the towns and villages that are noted for their old-world charm. These lodgings provide nice and friendly surroundings with their comfy rooms, hearty breakfasts, and attentive service.

- **Hostels**: In Tenerife, hostels are a well-liked choice for tourists on a tight budget or looking for a social environment. These reasonably priced lodging options provide private rooms, dormitory-style rooms, and public areas where tourists may mingle and exchange travel tales.

- **Camping and Caravan sites:** Tenerife has many camping and caravan sites if you prefer outdoor activities and have your own camping gear or motorhome. These facilities offer the opportunity to experience the natural beauty of the island as well as basic comforts.

- Tenerife is home to several all-inclusive resorts, especially along its southern coastline. These resorts provide a hassle-free vacation experience by offering comprehensive packages that include lodging, food, drinks, and a variety of activities and entertainment alternatives.

When selecting a place to stay in Tenerife, keep in mind things like location, accessibility to amenities and attractions, facilities and services offered, and price range. It is essential to make reservations in advance to ensure your preferred choice of lodging, especially during busy travel times.

Luxury Resorts and Hotels

Tenerife has a selection of opulent resorts and hotels that offer first-rate amenities, first-rate service, and breathtaking scenery. These businesses offer opulent and lavish experiences to discerning tourists. Here are a few of Tenerife's opulent resorts and lodgings:

- **The Ritz-Carlton, Abama**: This five-star resort is known for its opulent architecture, lovely grounds, and spectacular ocean views. It is located in Guia de Isora. The resort offers opulent accommodations and suites, numerous swimming pools, a championship golf course, a spa, and a selection of delectable eating options.

- **Gran Meliá Palacio de Isora**: This opulent beachside resort is located in Alcalá and features roomy villas with private terraces or balconies. Direct beach access, gorgeous infinity pools, a top-notch spa, gourmet dining options, and attentive service are all available to visitors.

- **The Royal Hideaway Corales Beach** is an adults-only resort in Costa Adeje that offers a calm atmosphere, a trendy and modern design, and spectacular sea views. The resort offers opulent suites with private terraces or pools, a spa centre, multiple swimming pools, and great dining establishments.

- **Baha del Duque** is a 5-star resort in Costa Adeje that combines contemporary elegance with traditional Canarian island architecture. The resort offers an opulent experience with lovely gardens, a private beach, numerous swimming pools, a spa, and a range of eating options.

- **Hotel Botánico & The Oriental Spa Garden:** This five-star hotel is known for its beautiful tropical gardens and breathtaking views of Mount Teide. It is located in Puerto de la Cruz. The hotel offers classy accommodations, a luxurious spa, lovely pools, and first-rate dining options, including a Michelin-starred restaurant.

- **GF Victoria:** This cutting-edge, green 5-star resort in Costa Adeje has opulent accommodations, breathtaking rooftop pools, a spa, and a variety of recreational amenities. The resort is renowned for its chic architecture, eco-friendly policies, and attentive service.

- Iberostar Heritage Grand Mencey is a historic 5-star hotel in Santa Cruz de Tenerife that combines elegance and contemporary conveniences. Beautifully furnished rooms, a rooftop pool, a spa, and several dining establishments, including a Michelin-starred restaurant, are all amenities offered by the hotel.

- **Selección Vincci La Plantacion del Sur:** This opulent boutique hotel is located in Costa Adeje and offers a serene, private environment surrounded by lush gardens. The hotel offers large rooms, a spa, numerous pools, and fine dining establishments to ensure a luxurious and restful visit.

The extraordinary comfort, amenities, and services offered by these five-star hotels and resorts in Tenerife enable visitors to have a truly opulent vacation. These places provide the ideal atmosphere for an amazing visit to Tenerife, whether you're looking for relaxation, excellent food, spa treatments, or spectacular vistas.

Budget Friendly Hotels and Hostels

There are several inexpensive hotels and hostels in Tenerife that offer cosy lodging without breaking the bank. These choices are perfect for tourists on a tight budget who nevertheless wish to stay in a nice and reasonable hotel. The following hotels and hostels in Tenerife are reasonably priced:

Hotels with Low Rates:

- Hotel Marte is a low-cost lodging option in Puerto de la Cruz that provides straightforward, comfortable rooms at reasonable prices. Its strategic location makes it simple to visit the town's landmarks and beaches.

- In the centre of Santa Cruz de Tenerife, the Hotel Adonis Plaza is a low-cost lodging option with modest amenities. It offers simple access to the city's eateries, stores, and attractions.

- In Playa de las Américas, the Hotel Sun Holidays is a low-cost lodging option with cosy accommodations and a prime position close to the beach and entertainment options. For people who want to visit the bustling resort region, it offers excellent value.

- **Hotel Tejuma:** This budget hotel, which is located in La Laguna's historic neighbourhood, provides straightforward, spotless rooms at reasonable prices. All of the city's attractions, stores, and restaurants can be reached on foot.

- **Hotel Rural El Patio:** This reasonably priced rural hotel is located in the charming village of

Garachico and offers comfortable accommodations in a traditional Canarian setting. It offers a tranquil getaway and is close to Garachico's picturesque streets and natural ponds.

Affordable hostels

- **Albergue Montes de Anaga:** This low-cost hostel is located in the Anaga Rural Park and offers dormitory-style lodging with modest amenities. It is a fantastic choice for hikers and outdoor enthusiasts who enjoy exploring the park's lovely pathways.

Youth Hostel Hostel La Terrera: Located in La Laguna, this hostel provides inexpensive dorm rooms and a shared kitchen. It is a fun and social lodging choice that is perfect for young, frugal tourists.

- In Puerto de la Cruz, the budget hotel La Playita offers both private rooms and dorm rooms at reasonable prices. It is conveniently situated in Puerto de la Cruz, near the beach, dining options, and activities.

- **Hostel Tenerife**: Located in Santa Cruz de Tenerife, this reasonably priced hostel provides cosy dorm-style lodging with a shared kitchen. For those on a tight budget who want to explore the capital, it is a practical choice.

- **Hostel Los Duendes Del Sur:** This low-cost hostel in El Médano offers reasonably priced dorm rooms close to the beach and windsurfing locations. It offers a relaxed atmosphere and is well-liked by fans of water sports.

These Tenerife hotels and hostels on a budget provide comfortable lodging without sacrificing affordability. They give you a practical starting point for affordably visiting the island's sights, beaches, and natural splendours.

Charming Bed and Breakfast

There are several wonderful bed & breakfasts in Tenerife that provide visitors with a warm and tailored experience. These B&Bs frequently claim distinctive locations, friendly hospitality, and a cosy environment. In Tenerife, check out these wonderful bed & breakfasts:

- **Casa Rural El Adelantado** is a beautiful B&B in La Orotava that is set in a renovated Canarian mansion from the 18th century. It has well-furnished rooms, a peaceful garden, and a comfortable sitting space. A nice breakfast with homemade delicacies is available for guests.

- The restored 17th-century **Casa Emblemática Garachico B&B** is located in the ancient village of Garachico. It provides a lovely courtyard, tastefully furnished rooms with classical accents, and a rooftop terrace with expansive views. Visitors can enjoy a delicious breakfast with regional cuisine.

- **Casa del Sol:** This beautiful B&B is surrounded by picturesque scenery and is situated in the town of Vilaflor. It provides cosy rooms decorated in a rustic style, a charming garden, and a terrace where guests can unwind and take in the tranquil ambiance. Every morning, a delectable home-cooked breakfast is provided.

- **El Patio de Tita**: This B&B is housed in a typical Canarian home and is located in the village of San Miguel de Abona. It has a gorgeous courtyard, inviting communal sitting space with a fireplace, and snug rooms with rustic charm. Visitors can begin the day with a full breakfast.

- **Casa Rural Los Lavaderos** is a rustic-style B&B housed in a 19th-century structure and is situated in Los Silos town. It provides cosy rooms with wooden furniture, a peaceful garden with a terrace, and a communal sitting area. Every morning, a fresh breakfast is provided.

- **Finca El Vergel Rural** is a bed and breakfast surrounded by lush gardens and vineyards in the rural neighbourhood of El Tanque. A gorgeous courtyard, comfortable rooms decorated in classic style, and a terrace with expansive views are all available. A tasty breakfast incorporating local ingredients is available for guests.

- The classic Art Nouveau-style structure that houses the Alhambra Boutique Hotel is located in Santa Cruz de Tenerife. It has tasteful, uniquely appointed rooms, a courtyard garden, and a comfortable sitting space. Every day, a continental breakfast is provided.

- Finca La Paz is a bed and breakfast with spectacular views of the Teno Mountains that is located in Buenavista del Norte. A lovely garden, a patio, and cosy rooms with rustic decor are all included. A continental breakfast using local, fresh products is available to visitors.

For visitors looking for a quiet and private lodging choice, these quaint bed and breakfasts in Tenerife offer a warm and welcoming ambiance, individualised service, and a distinctive experience.

Vacation Rentals and Apartments

Renting a holiday home or condo in Tenerife gives you the freedom, privacy, and opportunity to explore the island at your own speed. Vacation rentals provide a cosy and welcoming alternative to hotel stays for groups of friends and family or couples planning a trip. Here are some choices for flats and vacation rentals in Tenerife:

- Tenerife offers a wide range of villa rentals, from charming villas with private gardens to opulent homes with swimming pools and breathtaking ocean views. These villas frequently have many bedrooms, complete kitchens, and roomy living areas, offering plenty of space for families or parties.

- Rental flats are widely accessible in Tenerife, notably in well-liked tourist destinations like Costa

Adeje, Playa de las Américas, and Los Cristianos. These apartments come in a variety of sizes, from studios to multi-bedroom homes, and frequently include features like living rooms, balconies, terraces, and kitchens or kitchenettes.

- **Coastal condos**: If you want to live near the ocean, this is a fantastic alternative. These up-to-date, well-appointed apartments are frequently found in coastal developments, providing easy access to the sand and water. They frequently have swimming pools, common gardens, and are close to stores and restaurants.

- Rural Cottages: Rentable "casas rurales" or lovely rural cottages are available in Tenerife's interior, particularly in the island's north. These cottages are tucked away in gorgeous rural settings, surrounded by solitude and lush vegetation. They provide visitors a chance to relax and take in the island's pastoral beauty.

- **Apartments and townhouses** are available in a variety of vacation communities and complexes on the Canary Island of Tenerife. These neighbourhoods frequently have common facilities like tennis courts, swimming pools, and gardens, giving residents a resort-like feel.

- **Luxury Penthouse Rentals:** Tenerife has opulent penthouses that are available for rent for anyone looking for a taste of luxury. These penthouses frequently have roomy interiors, private terraces with panoramic views, and access to upscale amenities like spas, fitness centres, and swimming pools.

- Tenerife is home to eco-friendly getaways that place a strong emphasis on sustainability and the local environment. These lodgings frequently use eco-friendly building materials and have energy-saving technology. For individuals who want a more environmentally friendly stay, they provide an eco-aware experience.

- **Historic Apartments**: There are historical apartments for rent in towns like La Laguna and Santa Cruz de Tenerife. These apartments are frequently found in exquisitely restored structures, keeping the historical architectural appeal while providing contemporary comforts.

Think about things like location, ease of access to amenities and attractions, size and layout, and any particular features or amenities that are important to you when reserving a holiday rental or apartment in Tenerife. It is advised to reserve in advance, especially during the busiest travel times, to guarantee your preferred choice of lodging.

Camping and Caravan Sites

For outdoor enthusiasts looking for a more adventurous and natural-focused lodging choice, Tenerife has a number of camping and caravan sites. These locations offer chances to take in the natural beauty of the island and engage in outdoor sports. Tenerife offers the following campgrounds and RV parks:

- Santa Cruz de Tenerife's Camping Nauta is a well-known camping area with spaces for tents, campervans, and trailers. Showers, restrooms, and laundry facilities are available on the property. Due to its proximity to the city's heart, amenities and attractions are easily accessible.

- **Camping Montaa Roja**: Located in El Médano, this campground provides camping experiences close to the ocean. The campground offers campervan and tent sites, as well as amenities like showers, bogs, and a bar-restaurant. For those who enjoy the outdoors and water sports, it is the perfect option.

- **Camping Punta del Hidalgo**: This campground at Punta del Hidalgo provides breathtaking views of the ocean and a tranquil setting. Along with amenities including showers, stalls, and a canteen, it offers tent and campervan spaces. Exploring the coastline and hiking are both excellent nearby activities.

- **Cho Camping:** This campground is located in Cho and is tucked away in a rural area surrounded by greenery. Along with amenities like showers, stalls, and a bar-restaurant, it provides spaces for tents, campers, and caravans.

It is a great option for campers looking for peace and quiet.

- Camping Vilaflor offers a magnificent camping environment amidst pine forests and mountain vistas in Vilaflor, the highest hamlet in Tenerife. Along with services like showers, toilets, and a restaurant, the campground offers spaces for tents, campers, and caravans.

- **Camping Amarilla:** Located in Amarilla Golf, this campground is tucked away close to the water. Along with amenities like showers, stalls, and a bar-restaurant, it provides camping spaces for tents and campers. Golf courses and other recreational facilities are nearby the location.

- **Camping Valle Niza** is a campground near the beach that is situated in the town of Gümar. Along with amenities like showers, toilets, and a bar-restaurant, it offers spaces for tents and campers. Water sports and hiking are both possible in the neighbourhood.

When preparing to camp or park a caravan in Tenerife, it's crucial to review the particular rules and specifications of each site, including reservation procedures, amenities offered, and any extra costs.

It's best to bring your own camping gear, though some locations could let you rent it. While camping or travelling in a caravan in Tenerife, take pleasure in the island's natural beauty and show courtesy to fellow campers and the environment.

Unique Accommodations

Tenerife offers unusual and one-of-a-kind lodgings that give visitors extraordinary and unforgettable experiences. These lodgings offer a unique and engaging stay that goes above and beyond what is offered by conventional hotels. Here are a few unusual places to stay in Tenerife:

- Tenerife is well-known for its volcanic nature, and living in a cave house allows you to get a close-up look at the island's unique rock formations. These volcanic rock-carved cave homes provide a distinctive blend of rustic beauty and contemporary conveniences.

- **Treehouses**: Picture waking up in a comfortable treehouse surrounded by beautiful scenery and lush vegetation. Tenerife has treehouse lodgings where you can get back in touch with nature and take a tranquil escape far above the ground.

- **Igloos**: Although it may come as a surprise, Tenerife provides the chance to stay in igloo-like buildings that make for a comfortable and special experience. These igloo lodgings frequently have glass ceilings so that visitors can enjoy stargazing in the privacy of their own room.

- **Glamping Tents:** Tenerife offers glamping tents that give a deluxe camping experience for people who wish to be close to nature without sacrificing comfort. These large, luxurious tents provide private outdoor areas, attractive decor, and comfortable beds.

- Tenerife's coastline is littered with old lighthouses, some of which have been converted into interesting lodgings. You may take in the island's maritime heritage while staying in a lighthouse and take in the expansive ocean views.

- Tenerife is dedicated to sustainability and provides eco-friendly lodgings that have an emphasis on environmental preservation. These lodgings are built using environmentally friendly materials, run on renewable energy, and blend in beautifully with their natural surroundings.

- **Boutique Cave Hotels:** Tenerife's boutique cave hotels combine luxury with the special charm of cave homes to provide an unforgettable experience. These luxurious lodgings offer a really unforgettable stay because of its chic design, contemporary amenities, and stunning views.

- **Floating Hotels:** Visitors to Tenerife have the option of lodging on a magnificent boat or a floating home while visiting the island's ports. These distinctive lodgings offer a nautical experience and let visitors see the island's coastline from a different angle.

When making reservations for distinctive lodging in Tenerife, it's crucial to consider the unique amenities, services, and setting of each establishment.

These unusual lodgings frequently have limited availability and sometimes need reservations. During your trip to Tenerife, take advantage of the chance to stay in a setting that is genuinely extraordinary and make lifelong memories.

TASTES OF TENERIFE

Tenerife's Culinary Scene

The cuisine of Tenerife is a beautiful blend of local fresh ingredients, traditional Canarian dishes, and foreign influences. The island has a wide variety of dining establishments, so there is something to suit every taste.

Tenerife is a food lover's heaven, offering everything from native specialties to fresh seafood to international cuisine. Here's a look at Tenerife's food scene:

- Authentic Canarian cuisine, which is distinguished by its simplicity and use of regional products, is a specialty of Tenerife. A few delicacies you must try are sancocho (traditional fish stew), gofio (traditional roasted cornmeal), papas arrugadas (wrinkled potatoes eaten with mojo sauces), and mojo sauces (spicy or mild sauces made with garlic, peppers, and other spices).

- **Fresh Seafood:** Tenerife, an island, provides a wealth of fresh seafood. You may indulge in a range of dishes made with fish, prawns, octopus, and other locally obtained seafood, such as grilled fish, seafood paella, and seafood platters. Restaurants serving seafood are particularly well-known in the fishing communities and coastal towns.

- **Guachinches:** Exclusive to Tenerife, guachinches are unpretentious, family-run businesses that sell locally-produced cuisine and wine. These lovely restaurants provide hearty Canarian fare including roasted meats, and traditional stews, and offer a comfortable and genuine eating experience. Don't pass up the chance to go and sample Tenerife's cuisine.

- Tenerife also has a thriving international dining scene, which features fusion and other cuisines. There are many restaurants to choose from that serve food from different parts of the world, including Mediterranean, Asian, Mexican, and more. Tenerife has options to suit a variety of preferences, whether you're in the mood for sushi, pizza, or tapas with a contemporary twist.

- Tenerife has a long history of winemaking and produces top-notch wines from its vineyards. The peculiar aromas of the local wines are a result of the island's volcanic soil and special climate. You may try a selection of red, white, and rosé wines by visiting wineries and vineyards in areas like Tacoronte-Acentejo, Valle de la Orotava, and Abona.

- **Local Markets:** For food lovers, a trip to Tenerife's markets is a must. Both Santa Cruz de Tenerife's Mercado de Nuestra Señora de Africa and La Laguna's Mercado Municipal are well-known marketplaces where you can discover a broad selection of fresh fruit, regional cheeses, spices, and other gastronomic pleasures. The local culture can be experienced and the vendors can be talked to at these marketplaces.

- **Desserts & Sweets**: Tenerife's delectable desserts and sweets are perfect for satisfying your sweet appetite. Try the frangula (cornmeal and milk-based dessert), truchas de batata (sweet potato turnovers), quesillo (a creamy caramel flan), and bienmesabe (a classic almond-based dessert). These delights highlight the island's extensive gastronomic history.

The food scene in Tenerife offers a wide variety of delectable flavours, ranging from native Canarian fare to world cuisine. The culinary experience in Tenerife includes visiting guachinches, perusing the neighbourhood food markets, and tasting the fresh fish and wines produced on the island. Good appetite!

Traditional Canarian Cuisine

Tenerife's indigenous culture is firmly ingrained in traditional Canarian food, which is found across the Canary Islands. It depicts the geology, history, and accessibility of local ingredients on the island. The food is distinguished by its simplicity, seasonality, and use of fresh ingredients.

It also combines Spanish, African, and Latin American influences. When visiting Tenerife, you should taste some of these typical Canarian dishes:

- **Papas Arrugadas:** Small, locally grown potatoes are simmered in saltwater until they are soft, and the skin wrinkles in this traditional Canarian meal. Mojo sauces, which are tasty sauces made with garlic, olive oil, vinegar, and either red or green peppers, are frequently served with them. Mojo Verde (green mojo) is mellower than Mojo Rojo (red mojo), which is hotter.

- **Gofio**: Typically prepared from roasted and ground wheat or maize, gofio is a typical Canarian foodstuff. It has long been a mainstay of Canarian cuisine. Gofio is a versatile ingredient that may be used in a variety of meals, including gofio escalade (a hot porridge-like dish), gofio ambassador (a gofio-based dough), and as a garnish for soups and stews.

- **In Ropa Vieja**, vegetables including onions, peppers, and tomatoes are cooked with shredded beef, typically flank steak. Paprika, cumin, and garlic are used as seasonings. The dish's name, which translates to "old clothes," comes from the shredded, tattered-looking appearance of the meat.

- **Conejo en Salmorejo:** Conejo en Salmorejo is a typical rabbit dish and the rabbit is a common meat in Canarian cuisine. Before being stewed till tender, the rabbit is marinated in a mixture of spices, vinegar, garlic, and herbs. It is frequently served with mojo sauces and wilted papas.

- The Canary Islands are known for their traditional fish stew, known as "sancocho." It typically consists of boiled, salted fish (commonly cod), potatoes, sweet potatoes, and mojo sauces. A popular and soothing dish is sancocho canario, especially during holiday times.

- **Canarian puchero:** Puchero is a substantial one-pot stew made with a variety of meats, including beef, hog, chicken, and chorizo, as well as a variety of vegetables, including potatoes, carrots, cabbage, and chickpeas. It is a tasty and filling dish that displays the influence of Latin American and Spanish cuisines.

- **Bienmesabe**: Made with ground almonds, egg yolks, sugar, lemon zest, and cinnamon, bienmesabe is a typical Canarian dessert. It is frequently served chilled and has a creamy, slightly sweet flavour. Bienmesabe is an excellent way to finish a meal and sate your sweet tooth.

When visiting Tenerife, make sure to check out neighbourhood eateries and look for these typical Canarian meals. The gastronomic scene on the island provides a chance to sample the diverse flavours and rich cultural legacy of Canarian cuisine. Take advantage of Tenerife's culinary offerings!

Popular Local Dishes and Specialties

Many well-known regional dishes and delicacies that are adored by both locals and visitors can be found when exploring Tenerife's culinary scene. These recipes highlight the fresh ingredients from the island and the fusion of native Canarian flavours with outside influences. You should sample the following popular local foods and specialties when visiting Tenerife:

- Fresh fish is used in this meal, usually sea bass or sea bream, and it is fried in a salt crust. Fish that is delicate and tasty will have a salt crust that helps to lock in tastes and moisture. Regular accompaniments include Canarian potatoes and a dish of mojo sauce.

- **Churros de Pescado:** These bite-sized, crispy-fried fish fritters are known as churros de Pescado.

Fresh fish chunks are combined with a seasoned batter to make them, which is then deep-fried until golden brown. These savoury fritters are frequently eaten as an appetiser or tapas meal.

- **Carne Fiesta:** Carne Fiesta is a celebratory dish made of marinated beef or pork that is typically grilled or skewered. Garlic, herbs, and spices are used to season the meat, giving it a rich, smokey flavour. Mojo sauce and Canarian potatoes are typical accompaniments.

- A Canarian cheese dish known as queso asado is grilled or fried. Usually, semi-soft or semi-hard cheeses, like queso de cabra (goat cheese) or queso de flor (flower cheese), are used. The cheese is cooked to a melting point and a golden crust forms. It frequently comes with a side of mojo sauce or a drizzle of honey.

- Gofio (roasted and ground cereal grains) is combined with fish stock or animal broth to make the Canarian meal escalation de gofio. It often appears thick and porridge-like and is served as a side dish to dishes of meat or fish.

- Canarian quesadillas are distinct from the quesadillas you may be familiar with from Mexico. These are sweet pastries from Tenerife that are fashioned with flaky pastry and are filled with a sweet concoction of fresh cheese, sugar, and lemon zest. As a dessert or snack, they are released after being roasted till golden brown.

- The delicious delicacy known as Principe Alberto is made up of layers of chocolate sponge cake, sweetened cream, and almonds or hazelnuts. The cake is frequently decorated with toasted nuts and a thick chocolate ganache on top. Any sweet tooth will be satisfied by this well-liked dish.

When dining in Tenerife, look for these well-known regional delicacies and meals on the menus of quaint Canarian restaurants and diners. They provide a delicious dining experience and a sense of the island's culinary heritage. Enjoy discovering Tenerife's delicacies!

Seafood and Fresh Delights

Being an island bordered by the Atlantic Ocean, Tenerife is home to an abundance of fresh seafood and delectable dishes that highlight the wealth of the sea. Here are some seafood dishes and fresh treats you should taste when visiting Tenerife, from savoury shellfish to succulent fish:

- **Fresh Grilled Fish**: Indulge in grilled fish meals to sample the day's catch. Fresh fish is frequently marinated with herbs, olive oil, and garlic before being grilled to perfection, including dorada (sea bream) and lubina (sea bass). The straightforward cooking method lets the fish's inherent flavours show.

- Clams are cooked in a marinara-style sauce in this mouthwatering dish called almejas a la Marinera. White wine, garlic, parsley, and tomatoes are added to the clams as they steam, creating a flavorful and fragrant seafood treat. Don't forget to dunk some crusty bread in the tasty broth.

- **Gambas al Ajillo**: A well-known Spanish dish, gambas al ajillo is served in Tenerife. It comprises shrimp sautéed in olive oil, garlic, and hot peppers. The resulting meal is incredibly flavorful, spicy, and garlicky, and it goes great with toast or as a tapas alternative.

- **Caldo de Pescado:** Caldo de Pescado is a hearty and savoury traditional fish soup. A variety of fresh fish, including grouper, snapper, or cod, is simmered with vegetables, herbs, and spices to create this dish. The outcome is a flavorful stew that captures the essence of the sea and is hearty.

- Octopus on the grill, or pulpo a la plancha, is a well-liked seafood dish in Tenerife. The octopus is prepared by tenderising, seasoning, then grilling it to provide a tender, melt-in-your-mouth feel, and slightly charred skin. Potatoes, paprika, and olive oil are frequently added to the dish.

- Squid stuffed with a mixture of breadcrumbs, garlic, parsley, and occasionally regional cheeses is known as chipirones rellenos. After being cooked through on the grill or in a sauté, the squid is then served with a squeeze of fresh lemon juice. It's a delicious seafood alternative because of the fusion of flavours and textures.

- **Ceviche**: Despite not being a Canarian specialty, ceviche has grown in popularity in Tenerife thanks to its energising and bright flavours. The main ingredients in ceviche are usually raw fish or seafood that has been marinated in citrus juices like lime or lemon and combined with onions, peppers, and herbs. It gives a seafood sensation that is sour and zesty.

Visit regional seafood eateries and seaside communities noted for their fresh catches when exploring Tenerife's culinary scene. Your taste buds will be enticed by these seafood meals and fresh treats, which will give you a genuine sense of the island's seaside charm. Savour the delights of Tenerife while taking advantage of the ocean's richness!

Dining Experiences and Restaurants

From modest local cafes to luxury restaurants, Tenerife provides a wide selection of eating experiences where you may indulge in a variety of gastronomic delicacies.

Here are several dining establishments and restaurants in Tenerife worth checking out, whether you're looking for traditional Canarian cuisine, global cuisines, or creative fusion dishes:

- **Guachinches**: Go to a guachinche for a genuine, homey dining experience. These family-owned businesses provide regional wines and homemade fare. They provide a pleasant setting and frequently serve traditional Canarian fare including roasted meats, stews, and regional delicacies. The northern region of the island is where you may mostly see guachinches.

- **Restaurants serving seafood:** As an island, Tenerife is well-known for its seafood. For ocean-fresh fish, head to coastal communities like Los Abrigos, La Caleta, or Puerto de la Cruz. Investigate the seafood establishments in your area that offer a selection of grilled fish, paella, seafood platters, and classic Canarian seafood dishes.

- Tenerife has several restaurants with Michelin stars that provide great dining experiences. One of them is M.B., a restaurant with two Michelin stars that is housed in the Ritz-Carlton Abama. It displays cutting-edge cooking that combines regional cuisines with inventive methods. Kazan, a prominent Michelin-starred eatery with a reputation for serving modern Japanese cuisine, is another.

- The historic district of La Laguna is both a UNESCO World Heritage site and a popular dining destination. Cute eateries, cafes, and tapas bars adorn the pedestrianised streets. You can try Canarian specialties, visit the neighbourhood's gastronomic scene, and take in the vibrant ambiance of this cultural centre.

- **Santa Cruz de Tenerife**: The island's capital city provides a variety of food options. You can find a variety of culinary experiences here, from hip restaurants to classic Canarian diners. Particularly well-liked for dining is the city's waterfront district, which features contemporary architecture and beautiful scenery.

- Puerto de la Cruz is a coastal community renowned for its quaint ambiance and eating options. There are several restaurants to choose from that serve Canarian food, fresh seafood, international cuisine, and even vegetarian and vegan options. Take a lunch while admiring the ocean, and discover the town's diverse gastronomic options.

- **Wine Cellars & Vineyard Restaurants:** Tenerife has a thriving wine industry, and many wineries provide dining options in addition to wine tastings. Immerse yourself in the island's gastronomic and viticultural legacy by visiting vineyards and wine cellars in areas like

Tacoronte-Acentejo and Valle de la Orotava. Here, you may have a dinner paired with local wines.

Be willing to sample Canarian specialties, experience local cuisine, and enjoy the finest fish when dining in Tenerife. Tenerife's dining venues and restaurants offer unforgettable gastronomic excursions and range from hidden gems to well-known enterprises.

Vegetarian and Vegan Options

Tenerife is well renowned for its seafood and meat dishes, but the island is also expanding its vegetarian and vegan menu to accommodate a wider range of dietary needs. Here are some locations in Tenerife where you may discover delicious vegetarian and vegan options:

- Vegetarian restaurants and cafes can be found all around Tenerife, and many of them specialise in serving a variety of plant-based meals. Restaurants like "The Loving Hut" in Santa Cruz de Tenerife and "Restaurante El Mana" in Adeje offer a variety of menus with inventive plant-based cuisine, vegan burgers, salads, and wraps.

- Explore the various markets and health food stores that are located throughout Tenerife. Fresh fruits and vegetables, plant-based glasses of milk, tofu, and vegan snacks are among the vegetarian and vegan products that are frequently available in these establishments. There are options for making your meals and picking up wholesome snacks on the road.

- **Tapas and regional fare:** Vegetarian and vegan options are available, despite the traditional Canarian diet's predominance of meat and fish. Look for delicacies like veggie paella, pimientos de padrón (grilled peppers), and papas arrugadas (wrinkled potatoes) topped with mojo sauce. The restaurant may be able to meet your demands if you let them know in advance about your dietary preferences.

- Restaurants serving worldwide cuisine, frequently with vegetarian and vegan alternatives, are part of

Tenerife's diversified culinary scene. Restaurants like those in India, Mexico, Asia, and the Mediterranean, among others, frequently serve plant-based food. You can eat vegan-sauced pasta meals, falafel, sushi rolls, and veggie curries.

- **Vegetarian-Friendly Restaurants**: Many restaurants in Tenerife provide vegetarian and vegan options on their menus, even if they are not exclusively vegetarian or vegan. Look for menus that list vegetarian or vegan options, or ask the staff for suggestions and nutritional adjustments to fit your needs.

- Visit one of the many juice bars and smoothie stores spread out around Tenerife to stay energised and hydrated. These businesses provide a selection of smoothies, acai bowls, and fresh fruit and vegetable juices that are ideal for a nutritious and vegan-friendly snack or breakfast.

- **Street Food and Market Stalls**: Look for vegetarian and vegan options when perusing neighbourhood markets and food stands. For quick and filling plant-based snacks, look for stands serving grilled corn on the cob, fresh fruit cups, baked sweet potatoes, or falafel wraps.

Remember, it's always helpful to let the restaurant staff know your dietary preferences and limits so they can make accommodations for you. Tenerife's culinary scene is continually extending its selection of dishes for fans of plant-based cuisine in response to the rising demand for vegetarian and vegan options.

Canarian Wines and Beverages

Tenerife is well-known for its thriving wine industry, which creates a wide range of superb wines. Grape farming is made possible by the island's special volcanic soils, different microclimates, and distinct microclimates. Following are some Canarian wines and beverages to try while you're in Tenerife:

- Malvasia is a well-known white grape variety that is produced in Tenerife and other Canary Islands. It makes rich, aromatic wines with notes of flowers, honey, and tropical fruits. Malvasia wines are frequently savoured as an aperitif or coupled with seafood dishes. They can be dry or sweet.

- **Listán Blanco**: Another popular white grape type in Tenerife is Listán Blanco, usually referred to as Palomino. Wines with citrus tastes and floral aromas are produced that are crisp and pleasant. Wines from Listán Blanco are adaptable and go well with a variety of foods, such as salads, seafood, and light poultry dishes.

- **Listán Negro:** A red grape variety that is native to the Canary Islands is called Listán Negro. It generates medium-bodied red wines with distinct mineral characteristics, bright fruit flavours, and traces of spices. Grilled meats, roasted vegetables, and robust stews go nicely with Listán Negro wines.

- Tintilla is a less well-known red grape variety that is indigenous to Tenerife. With powerful flavours of crimson and black fruits, earthy undertones, and a velvety texture, it is used to make full-bodied, rich red wines. Tintilla wines are frequently matured in oak barrels, which gives the finished product more complexity.

- Palo Blanco is a rare and distinctive fortified wine made in Tenerife. It is produced with white grapes that have been sun-dried, usually, Listán Blanco or Malvasa, and it is matured for a long time in oak barrels. Rich flavours of almonds, caramel, caramelised fruits, and a tinge of saltiness can be found in Palo Blanco wines.

- Don't pass up the chance to experience Cerveza Canaria, the native Canarian beer, if you enjoy drinking beer. It is available in a variety of styles, such as lagers, ales, and craft beers, and it provides a cool way to quench your thirst as you explore the island.

- Hibiscus water, often known as 'Agua de Jamaica,' is a well-liked non-alcoholic beverage in Tenerife. Hibiscus blossoms are steeped in water to create this brilliant crimson beverage with a tangy and floral flavour. Refreshing alternative agua de jamaica is frequently served chilled.

Consider stopping by wineries and vineyards while you're in Tenerife to partake in wine tastings and discover more about the wine-making process.

Additionally, you may try and appreciate the distinct flavours and characteristics of Tenerife's beverages thanks to the wide variety of Canarian wines that are offered by numerous restaurants and bars on the island.

OUTDOOR ADVENTURES

Hiking and Trekking Routes

Tenerife has a wide range of breathtaking hiking and trekking paths that let you discover the island's varied topography and unspoiled beauty. Here are some well-travelled routes to take into account for your hiking activities in Tenerife, from volcano trails to coastal paths:

- **Teide National Park**: Mount Teide, the highest mountain in Spain, is a must-see for hikers. The top can be reached via several trails, including the well-known Teide Top Trail, which necessitates a permit. Roques de Garcia, one of the park's shorter paths, allows you to admire the unusual rock formations.

- **Anaga Rural Park:** Situated in the island's northeast, Anaga Rural Park is renowned for its luxuriant forests, wide gorges, and towering coastline cliffs.

  There are many hiking paths in the park, including the Circular Route of Afur, the PR-TF 9 trail to Chamorga, and the Los Organos Trail, which gives breathtaking sea-stack views.

- The Masca Gorge is a beautiful and difficult hiking trail that leads you through a small ravine flanked by high rocks. The walk starts in the community of Masca and descends to the shore while providing breathtaking vistas. Make sure you have the appropriate footwear and be ready for any steep areas.

- Explore the stunning La Orotava Valley, which is renowned for its luxuriant vegetation and ancient Canarian buildings. A well-liked trail that travels around the valley and passes by vistas, botanical gardens, and historical sites is called the Circular Route of La Orotava.

  It's a wonderful way to become fully immersed in the island's natural and cultural history.

- **Teno Rural Park:** Situated in Tenerife's northwest, Teno Rural Park features craggy cliffs, deep ravines, and breathtaking coastal vistas. The Teno Alto Loop, also known as the PR-TF 43 route, provides a chance to explore this breathtaking area. The path offers expansive views of the coastline while passing through quaint settlements.

- The Los Gigantes Cliffs are among Tenerife's most recognizable natural sights. You can take a trek along the coastal route that parallels the cliffs and provides breathtaking views of the enormous Atlantic Ocean and the towering rock formations.

  The route begins in the community of Los Gigantes and leads to Playa de Masca.

- Roque de los Muchachos is a notable summit that provides sweeping views over Tenerife and is situated in the Caldera de Taburiente National Park. You can take in the untamed volcanic environment and see the island's astronomical observatories by hiking to the summit. Keep in mind that the trail is difficult and can call for a permit.

It's crucial to be well-prepared and outfitted with the appropriate equipment, clothing, and supplies of food and water before setting out on any hiking or trekking expedition.

It's also a good idea to check the weather, the accessibility of the trail, and any required permits or restrictions. Choose a path that suits your fitness level and take in the stunning natural environment of Tenerife by hiking one of the island's many trails.

Scenic Nature Walks

Several routes let you fully appreciate Tenerife's natural beauty if you're searching for stunning nature walks that provide a more leisurely and laid-back experience. Here are some ideas for breathtaking nature hikes in Tenerife:

- **La Laguna Nature Park**: This park, which is close to the ancient town of La Laguna, features lovely walking pathways in an environment of lush vegetation, lakes, and botanical gardens. Take a stroll through the serene park's grounds to breathe in the fresh air and take in the variety of flora and fauna.

- **Rambla de Castro:** This dramatic stretch of shoreline in Tenerife's north gives breathtaking views of the sea. The walk traverses magnificent landscapes and historic terraces as it follows the Rambla de Castro's cliffs. With the calming sound of the waves and the cooling sea breeze, it's the ideal location for a peaceful stroll.

- **Punta de Teno**: A picturesque headland with rocky cliffs and expansive vistas, Punta de Teno is situated in the northwest part of the island. Enjoy a stroll along the seaside walkway while admiring the striking rock formations and the enormous Atlantic Ocean. Don't overlook the surrounding traditional village of Buenavista del Norte and the renowned lighthouse.

- **La Caleta to Playa del Duque:** Located in Tenerife's southwest, this seaside walk offers a relaxing stroll along the promenade with stunning views of the ocean and shoreline. The route passes via rocky coves and sandy stretches as it leads from the quaint fishing community of La Caleta to the well-known Playa del Duque beach.

- **Almond Blossom Route:** The Almond Blossom Route in Santiago del Teide is a lovely nature walk if you visit Tenerife during the almond blossom season, which is often in January and February. As you stroll through the lovely countryside, surrounded by a carpet of pink and white blossoms, take in the sight of blooming almond trees.

- **Los Tilos de Moya:** This natural reserve, which is part of the Moya municipality, contains a substantial laurel forest that goes by the name of Los Tilos de Moya. Discover the designated routes that meander through the dense woodland and provide shade and peace. Discover the area's rich biodiversity while listening to the birds sing.

- The promenade at Costa Adeje offers a relaxing stroll along the coast as it passes by stunning beaches, opulent resorts, and bustling seaside cafes. Take in the sunset, the ocean vistas, and the bustling ambiance of this well-known tourist destination.

These lovely nature strolls offer chances to commune with nature, take in the magnificent vistas of the island, and discover Tenerife's tranquil side. During your walks, keep in mind to bring a drink, wear comfortable shoes, and show respect for the natural environment.

Cycling and Mountain Biking Trails

With its varied terrain, beautiful routes, and ideal weather, Tenerife is a terrific location for cyclists and mountain bikers. Here are several cycling and mountain biking trails to check out in Tenerife, no matter if you like relaxing rides or exhilarating off-road excursions:

- **Teide National Park:** With breathtaking volcanic vistas as your backdrop, the routes that snake through Teide National Park offer an exciting cycling experience. Cycling is an excellent way to reach Mount Teide's summit, or you can simply explore the area to see the fascinating geological formations and breathtaking views.

- **Anaga Mountains:** In the northeastern region of Tenerife, the Anaga Rural Park has a network of paths ideal for mountain riding. It is an exhilarating location for off-road cycling because of the rough terrain, extensive forests, and challenging slopes. Select a route that suits your ability level from a variety of options while taking in the area's natural beauty.

- **Santiago del Teide**: Both road cycling and mountain bike enthusiasts will find beautiful routes in the Santiago del Teide municipality. Cycling through charming towns, vineyards, and breathtaking vistas allows you to take in the expansive views of the coast and mountains.

- **Orotava Valley:** With its lovely villages, verdant landscape, and scenic routes, the Orotava Valley is another fantastic location for cycling. As you cycle down the valley, you'll encounter lovely gardens, important landmarks, and typical Canarian architecture. There are both flat stretches and easy climbs along the trip.

- **Los Cristianos to La Caleta**: This coastal route connects Los Cristianos, a popular tourist destination, with La Caleta, a quaint fishing community. Take a stroll along the promenade and take in the breathtaking views of the sea and the shoreline. You can take a break at any of the cafes and eateries that are located along the route.

- **La Esperanza Forest:** The La Esperanza Forest, which is in Tenerife's north, has a network of mountain biking-friendly paths. While breathing in the clean mountain air, explore the woodland areas, ride through pine trees, and find secret valleys.

- **El Médano to Los Abrigos**: This coastline route offers a combination of paved roads and off-road tracks along Tenerife's southeast coast. Cycle via beaches, volcanic landscapes, and coastal cliffs from the well-known windsurfing hotspot of El Médano to the beautiful fishing community of Los Abrigos.

In Tenerife, it's crucial to observe safety precautions, use the necessary safety gear, and pay attention to traffic and road conditions when mountain riding or cycling. Additionally, take the weather into account and select routes that are appropriate for your level of fitness and competence. Tenerife offers a selection of paths to meet any cyclist's interests and abilities, whether you enjoy road riding or off-road excursions.

Water Sports and Activities

Tenerife is the ideal location for water sports and activities due to its beautiful coastline and crystal-clear waters. There are many possibilities, whether you're looking for heart-pounding thrills or just want to unwind and appreciate the seaside. Here are a few of Tenerife's well-liked water sports and activities:

- **Surfing**: Tenerife has world-class surfing conditions that draw surfers from all over. While more seasoned surfers can find tough waves at locations like Playa de Martiánez and Playa de Almáciga, beginners frequently surf at Playa de Las Americas and Playa de Los Cristianos.

- **Windsurfing and kitesurfing:** Tenerife is a haven for fans of windsurfing and kitesurfing thanks to its strong winds and ideal conditions. El Médano, on the southeast coast, is well known for its reliable winds, which makes it the perfect location for various water sports.

- **Jet skiing**: Rent a jet ski and race across Tenerife's glistening waves to get your heart racing. Jet ski rentals and guided tours are available in many coastal communities, including Playa de Las Americas and Los Cristianos.

- **Stand-Up Paddleboarding (SUP)**: While exploring Tenerife's shoreline, take in the tranquil and calming experience of stand-up paddling. You may glide through the tranquil seas and take in the stunning surroundings by renting SUP boards at several beachfront areas.

- **Kayaking**: Paddle a kayak along the island's coastline to uncover its secret coves, cliffs, and caves. In various coastal communities, including Los Cristianos and Los Gigantes, kayak rentals and guided tours are offered, providing a distinctive viewpoint of Tenerife's natural splendour.

- **Scuba diving and snorkelling:** Discover Tenerife's thriving underwater environment when scuba diving or snorkelling. Fantastic diving locations, including volcanic reefs, underwater caverns, and an abundance of marine life, can be found on the island. Popular destinations for diving and snorkelling excursions include Los Cristianos, Costa Adeje, and Puerto de la Cruz.

- **Fishing at depths**: Set out on a deep-sea fishing expedition with the hopes of landing a marlin, tuna, or other large game fish. There are many ports where fishing charters may be booked, making for a thrilling day on the open sea.

- **Whale and dolphin watching**: A variety of whale and dolphin species call Tenerife's waters home. Join a boat excursion or tour to see these wonderful animals in their natural environment. Marine life is abundant along the southwest coast, particularly around Los Gigantes and Costa Adeje.

- **Parasailing**: Try parasailing in Tenerife to feel the rush of flying over the waves. When you soar through the air while safely fastened to a parachute, you may take in beautiful views of the shoreline and the ocean.

- **Sailing and Catamaran Cruises:** Take a sailing or catamaran cruise along Tenerife's coastline to unwind and enjoy the sunshine. Swim in remote bays, take in the peace of the water, and get a fresh look at the island's breathtaking vistas.

You may engage in a variety of water sports and activities in Tenerife, but these are just a few. The island has a variety of activities to suit all interests and skill levels, whether you're a novice or an expert water enthusiast.

Whale and Dolphin Watching

It is a well-liked and unforgettable experience to go whale and dolphin watching in Tenerife, where you may see these amazing marine animals in their natural environment.

Diverse whale and dolphin species can be found in Tenerife's coastal waters, making it a popular vacation spot for lovers of marine life. The following information may help you understand whale and dolphin watching in Tenerife:

- **Best Time to Visit**: Tenerife offers year-round whale and dolphin watching excursions. The best time to see them, though, is typically from April to October, when the weather is warmer and the seas are more hospitable. The likelihood of spotting these marine creatures is greatest during this time.

- Whales and dolphins of various types can be found in the waters off Tenerife. The short-finned pilot whale, bottlenose dolphin, common dolphin, and Risso's dolphin are the most often seen species.

You might also get a chance to see other species like sperm whales and orcas, depending on the tour and the area.

- **Whale and Dolphin Watching Tours:** Tenerife is home to a sizable number of tour companies that specialise in whale and dolphin excursions. These excursions are led by knowledgeable guides who share their thoughts on the traits and behaviours of the marine creatures. Los Cristianos, Costa Adeje, and Los Gigantes are just a few of the coastal towns and ports from which the tours, which typically last a few hours, depart.

- **Boat Types:** A variety of vessels, including motorised boats, catamarans, and rigid inflatable boats (RIBs), are used for whale and dolphin watching cruises. The tour company and individual preferences may influence the boat selection. Catamarans are frequently chosen because of their stability and roominess, which offer a comfortable viewing area for marine life.

- **Responsible Whale and Dolphin Watching:** It's critical to select a tour company that upholds the rules and laws for observing marine species. Operators that value the welfare of the animals keep a respectful distance from them to reduce disturbance. Additionally, they offer instructional materials on marine conservation and the value of preserving these species' habitats.

- **Other aquatic Life:** Although the major goal of these tours is to see whales and dolphins, there is also a chance to see other aquatic creatures including sea turtles, flying fish, and different kinds of birds. The tour guides frequently give amusing details and knowledge about the local marine life.

To record your special moments, don't forget to pack the essentials like sunscreen, a hat, comfortable clothing, and a camera. It's a good idea to ask the trip operator about any special requirements or limitations as well as their cancellation policy.

You may experience a singular and respectful contact with Tenerife's remarkable marine species while supporting conservation efforts by choosing a reputable tour operator.

Golfing in Tenerife

Golf aficionados should visit Tenerife because it has wonderful courses with breathtaking scenery, agreeable weather, and a range of difficulties for players of all ability levels.

Tenerife offers a variety of golf courses to pick from, so you can play a round in beautiful surroundings whether you're an experienced player or a beginner. What you should know about playing golf in Tenerife is as follows:

- **Golf Courses:** Tenerife is home to a number of excellent golf courses that were created by well-known architects and are situated in gorgeous settings. Golf Costa Adeje, Golf del Sur, Buenavista Golf, Amarilla Golf, and Las Americas Golf are a few of the more well-known facilities. Beautiful seaside views, volcanic landscapes, and verdant fairways are just a few of the special qualities that distinguish each course.

- **Weather & Seasons**: Tenerife has a temperate, pleasant environment all year long, making it a great place to play golf all year long. The temperature is often between 20 and 25 °C (68 and 77 °F), which makes for pleasant playing conditions.

It is important to keep in mind that the weather on the island might differ between its northern and southern regions, with the latter typically experiencing warmer and brighter circumstances.

- **Golf Facilities**: Tenerife's golf courses provide first-rate amenities to improve your game. Fairways, practice facilities, driving ranges, putting greens, and professional golf academies are all regularly maintained on most courses. There are normally pro shops where you may buy golfing necessities or get help from professional employees, and you can rent golf clubs and equipment there.

- Golfers of all skill levels can play on Tenerife's golf courses, which provide a variety of attractions and difficulties. Beautifully crafted holes, bunkers placed with purpose, hazards involving water, and undulating greens are what you can anticipate. The island's volcanic landscapes are incorporated into some golf courses, while others provide picturesque ocean views.

- Tenerife organises a number of golf tournaments and events throughout the year that draw both professional and amateur golfers from across the world. These competitions provide you the chance to show off your abilities, play against other golfers, and enjoy the thrill of a competition in a breathtaking location.

- **Golf Resorts**: Many of Tenerife's golf courses are situated inside or close to golf resorts, offering golfers an all-inclusive experience. These resorts provide lodging, food options, spa services, and more recreational opportunities to make sure golf aficionados and their guests have a wonderful and restful stay.

- **Golf Lessons and Coaching**: Tenerife's golf courses frequently have skilled golf instructors and coaching programs available if you're wanting to enhance your golfing abilities or receive expert instruction. You can benefit from private lessons or group clinics to improve your game, whether you're a novice looking to master the fundamentals or an accomplished golfer looking to polish your stroke.

Tenerife offers golfers the pleasure of the game along with the beauty and comfort of the island's climate. Tenerife's golf courses offer an exceptional golfing experience in a truly stunning environment, whether you're an avid golfer or just play for fun.

Paragliding and Skydiving

Paragliding and skydiving are thrilling activities available in Tenerife, allowing thrill-seekers to soar through the air and take in breath-taking views of the island's surroundings. Tenerife offers the ideal setting for these thrilling activities, whether you're an expert paraglider or skydiver or a first-time explorer. What you need to know is as follows:

- Tenerife is a well-liked paragliding destination due to its varied landscape and good wind conditions. The island's breathtaking shoreline, mountains, and volcanic landscapes are perfect for paragliding.

  Tandem flights, where you can experience the excitement of paragliding while being accompanied by an experienced instructor, are offered by a number of paragliding schools and operators in Tenerife. These tandem flights are appropriate for novices and don't require any prior expertise.

- **Skydiving**: If you're looking for the biggest rush possible, skydiving in Tenerife is an amazing adventure. Skydiving is best done in Tenerife because of the island's clean skies, expansive vistas, and breathtaking shoreline scenery.

There are skydiving facilities in Tenerife that offer tandem jumps, where you'll be tethered to an expert instructor who will lead you through the entire experience, whether you're an experienced skydiver or this is your first time jumping. Safety is of the utmost importance, and the centres follow stringent safety regulations.

- **Training and Courses:** Tenerife has training programs and courses for various levels if you're interested in becoming a licensed paraglider or skydiver. Comprehensive instruction in ground handling, theory lessons, and solo flights are all offered by paragliding schools.

  Similar to this, skydiving facilities offer courses that walk you through the essential training to obtain a licence, including subjects like safety protocols, parachute control, and freefall methods.

- Operators of paragliding and skydiving in Tenerife place a high priority on safety and offer the required gear for these activities. When flying in tandem, you will be safely fastened to an experienced teacher who will operate the equipment and make sure you have a good time. The schools and facilities will offer the necessary gear, such as parachutes, harnesses, helmets, and other safety equipment, for people undergoing training or taking part in solo jumps.

- **Locations**: Tenerife has some beautiful spots for skydiving and paragliding. Flights over the southern coast, with its stunning beaches and cliffs, offer amazing views. Unique opportunities to soar over volcanic vistas are provided by the Teide National Park and the adjacent mountainous regions.

You'll be treated to breathtaking views whether you decide to skydive over the island's picturesque locations or go paragliding down the coast.

- **Weather**: Paragliding and skydiving in Tenerife are highly dependent on the island's weather. To guarantee that the conditions are ideal and safe for these activities, operators regularly check weather forecasts. Generally speaking, the island boasts consistent weather patterns, offering plenty of paragliding and skydiving possibilities all year long.

When participating in paragliding or skydiving, it's crucial to pay attention to your surroundings, heed safety precautions, and obey your instructor or guide's instructions.

These pursuits provide one a remarkable sense of independence and the opportunity to see Tenerife's natural beauty from a different angle. Paragliding and skydiving in Tenerife are sure to leave you with lifelong memories, whether you're an adrenaline addict or just looking for an unforgettable experience.

SHOPPING AND NIGHTLIFE

Shopping in Tenerife

Tenerife's shopping scene is vibrant and exciting, with a variety of options to suit all likes and inclinations. Tenerife offers options for retail therapy and one-of-a-kind bargains, with everything from crowded markets and shopping malls to lovely boutiques and regional craft shops.

What you should know about shopping in Tenerife is as follows:

- Tenerife is home to a number of contemporary shopping facilities and malls where you can discover a variety of stores, boutiques, and worldwide brands. Centro Comercial Plaza del Duque, Centro Comercial Parque Santiago, and

Centro Comercial Meridiano are a few of the well-known retail malls. Stores for clothing, gadgets, accessories, cosmetics, and other items are frequently found at these malls.

- **Traditional Markets:** When shopping in Tenerife, you must visit the lively traditional markets. These markets offer chances to buy one-of-a-kind souvenirs, handicrafts, and regional goods as well as a window into the local culture.

Two well-known markets where you can get fresh food, regional specialties, spices, crafts, and more are Mercados Municipales Nuestra Senora de frica in Santa Cruz de Tenerife and Mercados de Nuestra Señora de africa in Puerto de la Cruz.

- **Souvenirs and Regional Crafts**: Tenerife is well known for its regional craftsmanship, and the island is home to a wide variety of shops and boutiques that focus on offering distinctive souvenirs and locally created goods.

Be on the lookout for items like ceramics, leather goods, jewellery, Canarian-style apparel, and regional art. Unique items can be found in the craft stores in the municipalities of La Orotava, La Laguna, and Adeje.

- **Fashion and Clothing:** Tenerife boasts a variety of clothing stores and boutiques to suit different styles and budgets whether you're wanting to update your wardrobe or find the newest fashion trends. The bigger towns and retail malls offer a wide range of selections, from global names to regional designers. For fashion shopping, Santa Cruz de Tenerife and Playa de las Américas are particularly well-liked locations.

- **Duty-Free Shopping**: Tenerife is a desirable location for tax-free shopping because of its duty-free status. The airports include duty-free stores where you may buy a variety of goods, including alcohol, tobacco, fragrances, cosmetics, and gadgets. Tenerife South Airport is one such airport. Benefit from the reduced costs before leaving the island.

- Tenerife is a component of the Canary Islands, which are renowned for their distinctive regional products. Don't pass up the chance to taste and buy local delicacies including aloe vera products, wines, cheeses, and mojo sauce (a native Canarian condiment). These goods make wonderful presents or mementos to take back home.

- **Opening Times:** Although Tenerife's business hours can vary, they generally follow a similar schedule. The majority of businesses are open Monday through Saturday, with smaller towns taking a siesta at noon. Malls and shopping centres frequently have extended hours and are open all day. The bulk of stores are closed on Sundays and public holidays, but some tourist attractions and bigger supermarkets can be open.

- Remember to compare costs when buying in Tenerife, haggle at markets if necessary, and look into potential tax refunds for non-EU residents. Although credit cards are commonly used, it's still a good idea to have cash on hand, especially for smaller purchases or marketplaces that would prefer cash payments.

Shopping in Tenerife offers a lovely experience whether you're looking for clothing, regional crafts, mementos, or specialty goods.

Local Markets and Souvenirs

Tenerife is well-known for its thriving local markets, where you can get a taste of the local way of life, speak with welcoming merchants, and purchase one-of-a-kind items to bring back home. These marketplaces are a veritable gold mine of native goods, crafts, and genuine Canarian experiences.

Here are some well-known local markets where you can find one-of-a-kind mementos:

- Visit the Mercado Municipal Nuestra Senora de Africa in Santa Cruz de Tenerife if you want to experience local life firsthand. You can find stalls stocked to the gills with locally produced goods including Canarian cheeses and honey as well as an array of vibrant fruits, vegetables, and aromatic spices. Traditional goods including woven baskets, ceramics, and handcrafted fabrics are also readily available there.

- Puerto de la Cruz's Mercado de Nuestra Señora de África: This market, which is located in the city's centre, provides a lovely shopping experience. Investigate the booths selling regional produce, homemade jams, and fruits. Take advantage of the chance to sample and buy authentic Canarian delicacies like bienmesabe, an almond-based treat, and gofio, a roasted grain flour used in Canarian cooking.

- **Mercado del Agricultor (La Laguna):** The top local produce is displayed at this farmer's market in La Laguna. You can choose from a large variety of fresh and organic goods, including artisanal cheeses and seasonal fruits and vegetables. The market is also renowned for its herbal infusions, jams, and chutneys created from scratch. Additionally, you can peruse the kiosks selling locally manufactured crafts, leather products, and jewellery.

- **Feria Artesanal (Los Cristianos):** This craft market is an excellent place to find handcrafted goods. It is held every Sunday near the promenade in Los Cristianos. Look around the booths selling one-of-a-kind jewellery, pottery, woodwork, and traditional Canarian instruments like the timple. Local artists are also showing off their paintings and photographs.

- The lovely coastal village of Alcalá is home to the Alcalá Artisan Market, which sells a variety of regional goods and crafts. Admire the skill that went into making the unique leather products, beautiful pottery, and challenging lacework. Additionally, you might discover organic cosmetics manufactured from regional components like aloe vera or volcanic minerals.

- Tenerife has a wide range of possibilities for souvenirs that capture the spirit of the island and its scenic splendour. Look for products like hand-painted ceramics with regionally inspired designs, miniature versions of the famous Teide volcano, Canarian embroidery, traditional clothing, and so forth.

A bottle of regional wine or a jar of the typical Canarian condiment, mojo sauce, are two additional preferred keepsakes.

Always have an open mind while you browse the markets, engage with the merchants, and enjoy the bustling atmosphere. Although bargaining is uncommon in these marketplaces, polite interactions and sincere attention can frequently result in the discovery of hidden treasures or the learning of intriguing tales about the objects.

Tenerife's local markets provide shoppers the chance to discover one-of-a-kind souvenirs, support regional artists, and take in the rich cultural legacy of the island.

Shopping Centers and Mall

Tenerife has a number of contemporary malls and shopping centres where tourists may enjoy a wide variety of shopping experiences. These shopping areas provide a variety of worldwide brands, local boutiques, leisure activities, and food alternatives. Here are a few of Tenerife's well-known malls and shopping centres:

- This upmarket shopping mall, Centro Comercial Plaza del Duque, is situated in the Costa Adeje area and provides an opulent retail experience. High-end fashion labels, jewellery and watch stores, perfume boutiques, and designer shops can all be found in Plaza del Duque. Additionally, the mall features cafes, beauty salons, and fine eating establishments.

- Playa de las Américas' Centro Comercial Parque Santiago is a well-known retail centre that offers a variety of goods for different preferences and price points. A variety of foreign fashion labels, sports businesses, gift shops, and technology merchants may be found here. The mall also offers dining establishments, bars, and leisure activities like a movie theatre and a playground.

- Santa Cruz de Tenerife's capital city is home to Centro Comercial Meridiano, a sizable shopping complex that features a wide variety of stores. Visitors can browse fashion boutiques, home décor stores, beauty salons, and dealers of technology. Restaurants and fast-food companies are among the dining alternatives housed in the complex.

- La Villa's Centro Comercial provides a pleasurable shopping experience in a delightful location. La Villa is located in the picturesque town of La Orotava. The mall has a variety of bookstores, gift shops, and clothing and accessory retailers. La Villa also regularly organises exhibitions and cultural activities.

- El Trompo is a family-friendly retail centre in La Orotava. Its address is Centro Comercial El Trompo. It has a range of stores, including dealers of sporting goods, toys, and clothing. The facility also features a movie theatre, a bowling alley, and a kids' play area.

- Gran Sur is a well-known retail mall in Costa Adeje that features a variety of boutiques, eateries, and entertainment venues. Visitors can browse fashion boutiques, spas, sporting goods shops, and a sizable supermarket. The facility also has a movie theatre and a rooftop patio with expansive views.

These malls and shopping centres in Tenerife offer easy parking options, welcoming environments for customers to shop, and a variety of extras to make their shopping more enjoyable.

They also frequently hold events, exhibitions, and seasonal promotions, providing guests with a dynamic and interesting environment. Tenerife's shopping centres cater to a variety of preferences and guarantee a pleasurable shopping experience, whether you're searching for fashion, gadgets, souvenirs, or a place to unwind and eat.

Nightlife and Entertainment

The nightlife and entertainment scene in Tenerife is active and varied, providing a selection of options to suit various interests and inclinations. There is something for everyone, from hopping bars and clubs to live music places and cultural events.

Here are some of Tenerife's entertainment and nightlife high points:

- **Playa de las Américas:** This thriving tourist destination in Tenerife's south is well known for its exciting nightlife. A well-known area for bars, pubs, and nightclubs, the "Veronicas Strip" draws both locals and visitors looking to party all night long. You can listen to a variety of musical styles here, from popular songs to electronic music and live performances.

- **Santa Cruz de Tenerife**: Santa Cruz, the island's capital, has a wide variety of entertainment opportunities. The city holds several festivals and events all year long that include live entertainment, theatrical productions, and street acts.

  You may unwind with some cocktails and people-watching on Calle Castillo, a bustling area studded with clubs and eateries.

- Compared to the busy resorts, Puerto de la Cruz's quaint coastal town boasts a more relaxed nightlife scene. With its abundance of restaurants and cafes where you can relax with a drink while taking in the ambience, the Plaza del Charco neighbourhood is a well-liked location for nighttime strolls. In its theatres and public spaces, Puerto de la Cruz also presents cultural events and live music performances.

- **Adeje**: Adeje provides a variety of entertainment choices, such as hopping pubs and clubs, live music venues, and themed performances. The region is well-known for its well-liked dinner theatres, where you can eat while being entertained by Canarian folklore shows, cabaret acts, or flamenco performances.

- **Casino de Tenerife:** This elegant entertainment venue is situated in Santa Cruz and offers a glitzy experience. Enjoy a wonderful meal at the on-site restaurant, try your luck at the gaming tables or slot machines, and watch live entertainment in the casino's theatre.

- Tenerife is proud of its diverse cultural past, and you may witness traditional Canarian music and dance performances in a number of locations all over the island. Pay attention to traditional performances that include brilliant costumes, upbeat music, and spirited dances like the Canarian Joropo or the vivacious Carnival dances.

- Concert halls, restaurants, and beach clubs are just a few of the live music venues that Tenerife is home to. Local musicians as well as foreign artists from a variety of genres, including rock, jazz, reggae, and flamenco, will perform there.

- Tenerife boasts a number of karaoke and piano bars where people can show off their singing abilities or have a sing-along night out. These places offer a lively, engaging environment where you may sing along to your favourite songs or unwind to live piano music.

- It's important to note that Tenerife's nightlife is not exclusive to any particular regions or cities. Live music, themed parties, and cultural performances are just a few of the entertainment options available at many seaside resorts, hotels, and resort areas.

It's crucial to learn about local traditions and take the required security measures before enjoying Tenerife's nightlife. It's also advised to use public transportation or a designated driver to get back to your lodging safely.

Festivals and Events

Tenerife is well-known for its colourful and exciting festivals and events that highlight the island's rich cultural heritage and give visitors a taste of local customs and traditions. Tenerife celebrates a number of events all through the year, from vibrant carnivals to religious holidays and cultural displays.

Here are a few of Tenerife's well-known celebrations and events:

- The Carnival of Santa Cruz de Tenerife, which is regarded as one of the largest and most extravagant carnivals in the world, usually takes place in February or March. Street gatherings, lively parades, ornate costumes, music, and dancing are all featured. Both locals and tourists are drawn to the carnival because it offers a lively and happy atmosphere.

- Corpus Christi is a June religious event that is observed in a number of Tenerife towns and villages. The streets are adorned with exquisite carpets made of sand, flowers, and coloured salt that are arranged in lovely designs.

  There are processions and religious rituals that are accompanied by dancing and traditional music.

- **Romera de San Roque:** This annual pilgrimage honours the patron saint of the town and is held in Garachico in the month of August. Locals parade through the streets while bearing offerings and donning traditional Canarian clothing as part of a vibrant procession. Traditional food, music, and dancing are all part of the celebration.

- **Festival of the Virgin of Candelaria:** One of the most significant religious occasions in Tenerife is the Festival of the Virgin of Candelaria. It is observed at Candelaria on February 2nd and draws tourists from all across the island.

Fireworks, musical performances, traditional dances, and religious processions are all part of the event.

- The famous International Music Festival of the Canary Islands is held in January and February at various locations throughout Tenerife. It features a wide variety of musical acts, such as opera, symphony, classical, and modern music. This cultural spectacle features orchestras and renowned international performers.

- The International Tenerife Film Music Festival, also known as Fimucité, honours the craft of film music. It brings together artists, songwriters, and movie fans from all around the world. The program includes seminars, masterclasses, live orchestral film screenings, and concerts.

- Nature lovers can take part in the Tenerife Walking Festival, which typically takes place in May. Participants in this event can explore Tenerife's many landscapes, including the volcanic terrain and lush woods, through a variety of guided hikes and treks. It blends outdoor activity, cultural exploration, and delectable cuisine.

- **Feria de la Almendra (Almond Festival):** The Almond

Festival, which takes place in Santiago del Teide in February, honours the almond crop. Local almond-based treats like pastries, candies, and liqueurs are available for tourists to enjoy. The festival also features exhibitions, dance performances, and traditional music.

These are just a few of the numerous celebrations and events that take place all year long in Tenerife. Since they could change from year to year, it's a good idea to double-check the precise dates and locations of the events you're interested in. You can fully experience Tenerife's unique culture, traditions, and celebrations by taking part in these festivals and events.

Performance Arts and Theatres

With numerous theatres and locations that present a range of artistic acts, including theatre, dance, music, and more, Tenerife boasts a strong performing arts scene. There are options to satisfy diverse preferences, whether you enjoy live music concerts, modern dance, or classical theatre.

The following are some well-known theatres and performance spaces in Tenerife:

- **Tenerife Auditorium Adán Martin**: The Auditorio de Tenerife, which is situated in Santa Cruz de Tenerife, is a well-known architectural monument and a centre for the performing arts. Numerous events are held in this magnificent concert hall, including opera performances, ballets, theatrical productions, and concerts of modern music. The theatre is recognized for its superior acoustics and regularly welcomes orchestras and performers of the highest calibre.

- The Teatro Guimerá is a historic theatre from the 19th century and is located in Santa Cruz de Tenerife. It offers a varied lineup of theatrical productions, including comedies, musicals, dance acts, and dramas. Throughout the year, the theatre also offers musical performances, film screenings, and cultural gatherings.

- Santa Cruz de Tenerife's Espacio La Granja is a cultural hub that provides a stage for a variety of artistic expressions. Theatre shows, dance performances, musical performances, art exhibitions, and workshops are all part of it. Also held there are literary events, poetry readings, and author presentations.

- The Teatro Victoria is a historic theatre in Santa Cruz de Tenerife that presents a variety of theatrical productions, including dramas, musicals, and comedic shows. The theatre's schedule features both regional plays and touring performers, offering a diverse cultural experience.

- Located in Los Cristianos, Auditorio Infanta Leonor is a contemporary theatre that presents a variety of acts, such as plays, musical concerts, and dance performances. It gives both regional and international artists a platform, adding to the region's thriving cultural environment.

- The Teatro Leal is a historic theatre from the 19th century that is located in La Laguna. It hosts a range of cultural activities, such as theatrical productions, dance recitals, musical performances, and movie screenings. The performances are made more charming by the theatre's exquisite architecture.

- The Teatro Timanfaya is a well-liked location for theatre and live entertainment, and it is situated in Puerto de la Cruz. It offers a varied schedule that includes concerts, comedic performances, musical productions, plays, and more. The theatre additionally sponsors festivals and cultural activities that support local artists.

The theatres and performing arts centres in Tenerife are only a few examples. On the island, there are also a lot of hotels, resorts, and cultural institutions that occasionally stage performances and shows. You can plan your trip to Tenerife to see the thriving performing arts scene by looking at local listings, event calendars, and ticket availability.

Casinos and Nightclubs

Casinos and nightclubs are only a couple of the many entertainment options available in Tenerife's thriving nightlife scene. Here are some well-known casinos and nightclubs in Tenerife where you may dance the night away or try your luck at the gaming tables:

Casinos:

- **Casino de Tenerife:** This upscale and opulent gambling establishment is situated in Santa Cruz de Tenerife. It offers a variety of gambling alternatives, such as poker, roulette, blackjack, and slot machines. Regular poker tournaments and other special events are also held at the casino.

- **Casino Playa de las Américas**: This casino offers a vibrant and energising ambiance and is located in the well-known resort region of Playa de las Américas. It provides a range of gambling alternatives, such as poker, roulette, blackjack, and slot machines. The casino also has frequent live entertainment shows.

Nightclubs:

- Papagayo Beach Club is a well-known nightclub with a beachfront location and is situated in Playa de las Américas. There is a pool area, numerous dance floors, and a sizable outside terrace. The club features foreign DJs and plays a variety of music, including house, electronic dance music, and popular songs.

- One of the oldest and most renowned nightclubs on the island is called Tramps Tenerife, and it is located in Playa de las Américas. It has numerous rooms with a variety of music, including dance, R&B, and pop tunes. The club frequently holds themed gatherings and special occasions.

- Playa de las Américas's Monkey Beach Club provides a distinctive seaside clubbing experience. It has a big terrace outside, a swimming pool, and a dance floor with a variety of music, such as house, reggaeton, and Latin beats. Live performances and themed events are also held at the club.

- Achaman Discopub is a well-known nightclub in Puerto de la Cruz that is renowned for its energetic ambiance. It offers a variety of musical genres, such as Latin, reggaeton, and pop tunes. Live music performances and special events are frequently held at the club.

- **Faro Chill Art:** Housed in a structure designed like a lighthouse and situated in Costa Adeje, Faro Chill Art is a chic nightclub. It features a rooftop terrace, a large dance floor, and breath-taking ocean views. House, techno, and electronic music are among the genres played in the club.

It's crucial to be aware that Tenerife's casinos and nightclubs may have different operation schedules and admission requirements. Some places can have age restrictions and clothing requirements. To ensure a fun and hassle-free trip, it is advised to double-check the specifics and make plans accordingly.

PRACTICAL TIPS AND SAFETY

Health and Safety Information

Prioritising your health and safety is vital when visiting Tenerife. Observe the following important health and safety information:

- Make sure you have adequate travel insurance before you leave, which should cover medical emergencies, trip cancellation or interruption, lost or stolen belongings, and other contingencies.

- Hospitals and clinics, as well as other medical facilities, are available on the Canary Island of Tenerife. For rapid assistance in a medical emergency, use the 112 emergency hotline throughout Europe.

- **Immunizations**: Before visiting Tenerife, inquire with your doctor or a travel clinic about any vaccines that may be advised. Regular vaccinations against diseases like influenza, diphtheria, tetanus, and pertussis are generally advised.

- Sun protection is essential because Tenerife has a sunny environment and the sun's rays can cause skin cancer. During the most intense sun exposure, apply sunscreen with a high SPF, sunglasses, and a hat, and seek cover from the sun.

- Stay hydrated by drinking plenty of water, especially in warm weather. Bring a bottle of water with you and fill it up as necessary.

- Generally speaking, Tenerife's tap water is safe to drink. However, bottled water is easily accessible and can be purchased if you like.

- Food Security: Tenerife has a vast selection of delectable cuisine. Make sure you eat meals from recognized restaurants and practise good cleanliness. Before eating, wash your hands, and stay away from raw or undercooked food.

- Keep up with the most recent COVID-19 recommendations and any travel limitations imposed by the local government and your country of residence. Respect hygiene rules, use masks when necessary in public settings, and maintain social distance as needed.

- Save crucial phone numbers, such as those for your local emergency services, your embassy or consulate, and your travel insurance company, in case of emergencies.

- Although Tenerife is often secure for travellers, it is still advisable to exercise common sense care. Be mindful of your surroundings, protect your possessions, and steer clear of dark, lonely regions at night.

For the most recent health and safety information relevant to your trip, it is advised to examine official government websites and travel advisories. You can guarantee a secure and happy journey to Tenerife by being informed and following the required safety precautions.

Emergency Contacts

Here are some crucial numbers to know in Tenerife in case of an emergency:

- Emergency Services (Fire, Medical, and Police): 112
- In the event of any emergency, including those involving the police, fire, or medical personnel, call emergency number 112.

- 062 Local Police (Civil Guard)
  For non-emergency situations requiring police assistance, call the Guardia Civil, the local police, at this number.

- Police for Travelers: 902 102 112
  The tourism police have received special training to help travellers. They can communicate in various languages and offer advice, assistance, and support.

- Emergency Medical Services: Dial 112 For any urgent medical assistance needed, dialling 112 will link you to emergency medical services.

- 111 ambulance
Dialling 112 will link you to the right emergency medical services if you need an ambulance due to a medical emergency.

- Bomberos Fire Department: 112
Call the fire department at 112 if you see a fire or need help in a situation involving a fire.

- Protection Civil: 922 231 000
During natural catastrophes or major emergencies, Civil Protection is in charge of emergency management and aid.

- Embassy or Consulate: It's crucial to have your embassy or consulate's contact information on hand in case you need assistance or support. For assistance, get in touch with the embassy or consulate of your home nation in Spain.

- Remember that emergency phone numbers can change or vary over time. For the most recent emergency contact information, it is important to check with your housing provider or the local authorities.

When reporting an emergency, keep in mind to be specific and exact with your information and to stay on the line until the emergency service operator tells you to hang up.

Local Customs and Etiquette

Understanding the regional customs and manners can help you have a respectful and happy trip to Tenerife. To remember, have the following in mind:

- A handshake and a cordial "Hola" (hello) or "Buenos das" (good morning) are appropriate greetings during the day. A kiss on each cheek may be given as a greeting in more casual contexts.

- Tenerife has a loose attitude toward punctuality, therefore being a few minutes late to social events is fine. Being on time for formal occasions and business meetings is still advised.

- Due to its mild temperature, Tenerife has a generally informal dress code. Most situations can be dressed up or down, although more formal wear may be required in posh restaurants, theatres, or at special events.

- Tenerife has several churches and other religious buildings, thus it's necessary to dress modestly and with respect when visiting these locations. You should also cover your shoulders and wear modest apparel.

- **Tipping**: Although not required in Tenerife, it is appreciated for excellent service. If you are pleased with the service at a restaurant or by a cab driver, it is normal to leave a little tip (often between 5 and 10% of the entire price).

- Spanish is the official language in Tenerife. Even though many residents in tourist destinations are English speakers, it is courteous to learn a few fundamental Spanish words or utilise a translation app while speaking with people.

- Tenerife is known for its stunning natural surroundings, thus it's crucial to respect nature and the environment. Follow established hiking pathways, refrain from littering, and obey any rules or regulations in protected areas.

- Like many regions of Spain, Tenerife practises the siesta custom, in which stores and establishments may close for a few hours in the afternoon. Planning your activities appropriately and being aware of probable closures during nap hours is beneficial.

- **Beach etiquette**: It's crucial to respect the environment and fellow beachgoers when using Tenerife's beaches. Use the specified swimming areas, heed any safety warnings, and tidy up by properly disposing of any rubbish.

- **Photography**: It is polite to first obtain permission from locals before taking any pictures of them. It's crucial to observe any limits on photographs, especially if they apply to religious rituals or private gatherings.

You can make the most of your time in Tenerife and foster beneficial interactions with the locals by adhering to these traditions and demonstrating respect for the community.

Tipping and Bargaining

Here are some suggestions to keep in mind when tipping and haggling in Tenerife:

Tipping:

- **Cafés and restaurants**: Although tipping is not required at restaurants, it is appreciated for exceptional service. Leaving a little tip, typically between 5 and 10% of the total amount, is customary, especially when the service has been great. Before leaving a tip, confirm whether a service fee was added to the bill at the restaurant.

- **Bars**: If the bartender provided excellent service, it is usual to round up the tab or offer a modest gratuity. This might be a couple of cents or an extra 5–10% of the overall amount.

- **Hotels**: Although tipping hotel employees is not required, doing so shows your appreciation for their superior service. If the concierge or housekeeping staff went above and beyond to help you, you can leave them a little tip.

- **Taxis**: Although tipping is not required, it is customary to round up the fare as a sign of gratitude for the service received.

Bargaining:

- **Markets and Street sellers**: Bargaining is frequently done at local markets, especially when purchasing souvenirs, crafts, and other items from street sellers. Nevertheless, it's crucial to act with decency and keep a positive outlook while negotiating.

- **Retail Stores:** at Tenerife, bargaining is uncommon at retail stores and shopping malls. Prices are typically predetermined, so trying to bargain for a lesser price might not go down well.

- **Excursions and Tours:** The cost of scheduled excursions and tours is often predetermined. However, if you're in a group or travelling during off-peak hours, you might be able to bargain for a lower rate. If there is an opportunity for bargaining, it is worth politely asking.

- Keep in mind to bargain cordially and respectfully. It's critical to keep the seller's livelihood in mind and avoid negotiating a price that is too low. Accept the price as is if the vendor won't budge, or think about looking elsewhere.

In general, bargaining is mostly restricted to marketplaces and street sellers, while tipping is valued in some circumstances. The majority of the time, prices are predetermined, and haggling is not typical.

Transportation Tips

Here are some suggestions for getting around Tenerife effectively when it comes to transportation:

- Buses and trams are part of the dependable public transportation system in Tenerife. The most popular form of public transportation on the island, buses connect all areas. To locate bus stops, look for the green "Guagua" signage. Santa Cruz and La Laguna have a tram service. Use a reloadable transit card or buy tickets directly from the driver for convenience.

- Renting a car is a popular option in Tenerife, particularly if you want to explore the island on your own. There are many automobile rental companies to choose from, so it's better to reserve in advance to get the best deals. Keep in mind to have a current driver's licence and become acquainted with the local traffic laws.

- **Taxis**: In Tenerife, taxis are frequently available and can be found at designated taxi stands or flagged down on the street. Taxis use metres, and the cost is determined by the travel distance and the waiting time. It's a practical choice if you want door-to-door transportation or for brief distances.

- **Uber and ride-sharing:** Tenerife has access to Uber, which offers a substitute for conventional taxis. Through smartphone apps, users can access ride-sharing services, and prices are typically established in advance.

- **Riding**: For those who enjoy riding, Tenerife has stunning scenery. You may either sign up for organised cycling trips or rent bicycles from a variety of rental shops. For safety, be aware of the state of the roads and select designated bike lanes or calmer routes.

- **Ferries**: If you want to travel between islands in the Canary Islands, ferries are your best option. Santa Cruz and Los Cristianos are the locations of Tenerife's primary ferry terminals. Checking the ferry timetables and purchasing tickets in advance is advised, especially during periods of high travel demand.

- **Parking**: If you decide to rent a car, be aware of the rules regarding parking. Parking zones with specific regulations and costs can be found in many towns and cities. To avoid tickets or towing, pay attention to the signage and use parking lots or garages where they are available.

- Tenerife drives on the right side of the road, and posted speed limits are in kilometres per hour. In rural places, be careful on curving, narrow roads. Plan because parking spaces in busy tourist destinations may be scarce.

- **Prepare for Peak Travel Times:** Popular destinations may be crowded and traffic may be intense during peak tourist seasons, such as the summer and significant holidays. To avoid crowds, think about altering your travel schedule or getting there early.

- Use maps or navigation tools to plan your travels, especially if you're trekking or exploring distant locations. Offline maps might be helpful in remote locations where mobile network service may be spotty or nonexistent.

You can make the most of your time in Tenerife and travel the island with ease to discover its many attractions by taking into account these transportation suggestions.

Packing Essential

It's crucial to pack thoughtfully for your vacation to Tenerife and to include products that are necessary for a relaxing and pleasurable stay. The following items are a must-pack for your trip to Tenerife:

- **Pack lightweight**, breathable clothing like T-shirts, shorts, sundresses, and skirts because Tenerife has a mild, warm temperature. For chilly evenings or trips to higher altitudes, pack a few long sleeve shirts or thin layers.

- **Swimwear** is a must-pack item because Tenerife is known for its stunning coastline and beaches. You'll have plenty of chances to cool off in the ocean or unwind by the pool, whether you're wearing a swimsuit, bikini, or swim trunks.

- Pack your must-have sun protection goods because Tenerife's sun can be very intense. For additional sun protection, carry high-SPF sunscreen, sunglasses, a wide-brimmed hat, and a light, long-sleeved cover-up.

- Pack comfortable shoes because Tenerife provides a variety of outdoor activities and exploration options. Walking along coastal roads, trekking, or exploring natural areas is best done in sneakers or walking shoes. For informal activities and trips to the beach, sandals or flip-flops are ideal.

- **Daypack or Beach Bag**: When venturing out for the day, a lightweight daypack or beach bag comes in helpful for transporting necessities like sunscreen, water bottles, towels, snacks, and personal things.

- **Medication and First Aid Kit:** Pack enough prescription medication to last the duration of your vacation if you take any. Bring a basic first aid package as well, including bandages, painkillers, antiseptic cream, and any personal drugs you might need.

- **Travel adapters:** To recharge your electronic gadgets while visiting Tenerife, keep in mind that the island uses Euro Plug (Type C) and Schuko (Type F) power outlets.

- **Airline Documents**: Don't forget to pack your passport or other form of identification, as well as any necessary airline tickets, hotel bookings, and information about your travel insurance. Having digital versions of these documents safely kept on your phone or in cloud storage is also beneficial.

- Cash and other forms of payment: Although credit cards are generally accepted in Tenerife, it's always a good idea to have some cash on hand for smaller transactions, gratuities, and unexpected expenses. To prevent any problems with card usage, be sure to let your bank know about your vacation intentions.

- **Entertainment and electronics**: If you like to read, bring along a book or e-reader for downtime entertainment. Using a camera, smartphone, or tablet to record memories, navigate, and stay connected are some other handy technologies.

Before you pack, be sure to look up the Tenerife weather prediction so you can get a better idea of what to expect. You will be well-prepared to take advantage of everything Tenerife has to offer if you bring these necessities.

Travel Insurance

Travel insurance is a crucial component of trip preparation since it offers coverage and financial security in the event of unforeseen circumstances or crises while you are away from home. Here are some important considerations to bear in mind when thinking about travel insurance for your trip to Tenerife:

- **Medical Coverage**: Search for a travel insurance plan with complete medical protection. If you are sick or hurt while travelling, this should pay for medical costs, emergency medical evacuation, and repatriation. Make sure the coverage limitations are adequate for your requirements.

- Travel insurance can offer coverage for trip cancellation or interruption brought on by unforeseeable events like illness, injury, or other covered reasons. This can assist in reimbursing non-refundable costs including airfare, lodging, and reserved activities.

- **Baggage and Personal Property**: Take into account purchasing insurance that covers lost, stolen, or damaged luggage as well as personal property. This can assist in covering the expense of replacing important things or compensating for delayed baggage.

- **Trip Delays**: If there are severe delays in your trip plans, your travel insurance may be able to pay for additional lodging or meals. Details on coverage and any time restrictions should be found in the policy.

- Search for a policy that provides emergency support services around-the-clock. In the event of unexpected events like medical problems, travel delays, or other unforeseen circumstances, this can offer support and direction. These services can be really helpful, especially if you're travelling somewhere new.

- **Pre-Existing Medical Conditions**: It's crucial to disclose any pre-existing medical conditions when buying travel insurance. While some policies may have exclusions or charge higher premiums, others might cover pre-existing diseases. To fully comprehend the coverage offered, thoroughly review the policy terms and conditions.

- **Activities and Adventure Sports:** Verify that your travel insurance will cover any activities or adventure sports you choose to partake in while visiting Tenerife. Check the policy specifics and, if necessary, consider getting additional coverage as some policies may contain exclusions for specific high-risk activities.

- **Policy Exclusions:** Spend some time studying the policy's restrictions, criteria, and exclusions. Making an informed choice and avoiding unexpected outcomes requires an understanding of what is covered and what is not.

- **Compare Quotes and Coverage**: To select a travel insurance policy that best satisfies your demands and budget, it is advisable to compare quotes and coverage from several travel insurance providers. When making your choice, take into account the coverage limits, deductibles, and client testimonials.

- **Study the Policy Documents & Keep a Copy:** Before your journey, carefully study the policy documents & bring a copy with you. Learn about the claims procedure and who to contact in case of emergency.

Keep in mind that purchasing travel insurance is a crucial investment that can give you financial security and peace of mind while you're visiting Tenerife. It's crucial to pick insurance that complements your unique travel schedule and provides the coverage you need.

Essential Useful Phrases

You can use the following words and phrases to communicate in Tenerife:

- Hello - Hola
- Good morning - Buenos días
- Good afternoon - Buenas tardes
- Good evening - Buenas noches
- Thank you - Gracias
- You're welcome - De nada
- Excuse me - Perdón/Disculpe
- Please - Por favor
- Yes - Sí
- No - No
- I don't understand - No entiendo
- Can you help me? - ¿Puede ayudarme?
- Where is...? - ¿Dónde está...?
- How much does it cost? - ¿Cuánto cuesta?
- I would like... - Me gustaría...
- Do you speak English? - ¿Habla inglés?

- I need a doctor - Necesito un médico
- Where is the bathroom? - ¿Dónde está el baño?
- Cheers! - ¡Salud!
- Goodbye - Adiós

Remember to talk slowly and clearly, and if you're not comfortable using words or gestures, don't be scared to do so. The locals will value your attempt at communication and be delighted to help you.

DAY TRIPS AND EXCURSIONS

Nearby Islands and Attractions La Gomera

In the archipelago of the Canary Islands, La Gomera is an adjacent island to Tenerife. La Gomera, which is well-known for its lush surroundings, rough mountains, and lovely villages, provides a distinctive and relaxing getaway.

The following are some sights and things to do on the island:

- A must-see place in La Gomera is Garajonay National Park, which is also a UNESCO World Heritage site. This ancient laurel forest is home to beautiful vistas with expansive views of the island, hiking routes, and lush vegetation.

- Playa de Valle Gran Rey is one of the stunning beaches in Valle Gran Rey, a gorgeous valley on La Gomera's west coast. Swimming, snorkelling, diving, and other water sports are all quite popular in the region.

- **Agulo**: This quaint town built on La Gomera's cliffs provides stunning views of the Atlantic Ocean and other islands. Visit the Church of San Marcos, stroll through the winding lanes, and unwind in the peaceful ambiance of the town.

- **San Sebastián de La Gomera**: San Sebastián, the capital of La Gomera, has historical value because Christopher Columbus stopped here on one of his trips. Explore the historic quarter, which is home to the 15th-century tower

Torre del Conde, and take in the vibrant architecture and energetic ambiance.

- Playa Santiago is a peaceful seaside community with a lovely harbour that is situated on La Gomera's southern shore. Enjoy the calm beach, take a stroll down the promenade, and indulge in local eateries' excellent seafood.

- The famous Mirador de Abrante gives expansive views of the island, the nearby Tenerife volcano Teide, and the Atlantic Ocean. It has a distinctive glass platform that juts out over the cliffs and offers an exhilarating experience.

- Due to its proximity to the seas of the Atlantic Ocean, which are abundant with marine life, La Gomera is an excellent site to go whale watching. Join a boat tour for the chance to see different whale and dolphin species.

- Enjoy the local cuisine of La Gomera, which features delicacies like gofio (toasted cornmeal), almogrote (a cheese and garlic spread), and fresh fish dishes. Discover the regional cuisine by dining at the neighbourhood establishments.

You can take a ferry from Los Cristianos in the south of Tenerife to La Gomera from Tenerife. The ferry voyage lasts for around an hour. It's a good idea to research ferry timings beforehand and make travel arrangements appropriately. La Gomera offers a serene and unspoiled getaway where you may fully appreciate the distinctive scenery and indigenous island culture.

Mount Teide National Park

On the island of Tenerife in the Canary Islands, Spain is the well-known natural attraction known as Mount Teide National Park. The tallest stratovolcano in Spain, Mount Teide, is located there. The following are some noteworthy sights and things to do in Mount Teide National Park:

- **Mount Teide**: At an astounding 3,718 metres (12,198 feet) above sea level, Mount Teide serves as the centrepiece of the national park. It is a well-known representation of Tenerife and its peak provides stunning panoramic views. With a permit, you can trek to the summit or ride a cable car to take in the breathtaking views.

- The well-known national park rock structure known as Roques de Garcia is distinguished by its remarkable volcanic forms. The most well-known rock is Roque Cinchado, which is frequently shown in pictures and postcards highlighting Tenerife's distinctive scenery.

- **Teide Observatory:** One of the top astronomical observatories in the world, the Teide Observatory is situated inside the national park. Visitors can learn about astronomy through guided tours and exhibitions, and it is home to a variety of telescopes and research facilities.

- **Landscapes resembling the Moon or Mars**: With its wide lava fields, craggy rock formations, and unusual flora that has adapted to the harsh environment, Mount Teide National Park's volcanic landscapes are reminiscent of a lunar or Martian landscape. It is fascinating and strange to explore these regions.

- A simple alternative to a taxing climb, the Mount Teide cable car makes it possible to ascend the summit and take in the surrounding scenery. Visitors can enjoy breathtaking views of the national park and the nearby islands as the cable car brings them quite close to the summit.

- **Trails for Hiking**: Many hiking trails in Mount Teide National Park are appropriate for people of all fitness levels and interests. There are routes accessible to explore the park's various landscapes, volcanic structures, and endemic flora and animals, whether you choose a stroll or a strenuous excursion.

- **Stargazing**: Mount Teide National Park is a great place to see the night sky due to its pristine skies and low levels of light pollution. The park has been classified as a Starlight Reserve, and you may take advantage of planned stargazing excursions and programs to see the beautiful night sky.

- **Flora and Fauna:** Despite the national park's severe volcanic environment, a wide range of plant and animal species have adapted to it. Keep an eye out for unusual plant life, such as the Teide bugloss and Canary Island pine trees, as well as bird species, such as the blue chaffinch and Berthelot's pipit.

It's vital to keep in mind that certain sites can need permits or have limited access due to Mount Teide National

Park's protected status. For a secure and pleasurable visit, it is advised to review the park's rules, make preparations, and take into account guided tours or professional guidance.

Los Gigantes Cliffs

On the western coast of Tenerife, one of the Canary Islands in Spain is the Los Gigantes Cliffs or Acantilados de Los Gigantes in Spanish. What you should know about these stunning cliffs is as follows:

- **Impressive grandeur:** The Los Gigantes Cliffs, which rise to 800 metres (2,600 feet) vertically from the ocean, are renowned for their impressive grandeur. The Atlantic Ocean's brilliant blue waters are a magnificent contrast to these towering rocks.

- The cliffs' geological formation is the product of millions of years of erosion following previous volcanic activity. The sheer vertical walls and craggy basalt formations are magnificent to see.

- **Landmark**: The Los Gigantes Cliffs is a well-known destination for tourists to Tenerife and has earned the title of the island's iconic landmark. They are a popular location for tourists and photography because of their magnificence and sheer size.

- **Marine Life:** The cliffs are stunning below the water as well as above it. Due to the abundance of marine life in the area, Los Gigantes is a fantastic location for diving and snorkelling. There's a chance you'll see dolphins, whales, and other aquatic animals nearby.

- **Boat Tours:** Taking a boat trip is one of the greatest ways to fully experience the grandeur of the Los Gigantes Cliffs. Many businesses provide guided excursions that let you approach the cliffs up close, sail at their base, and take in their impressive height.

- **Water sports**: The vicinity of the cliffs offers opportunities for kayaking, jet skiing, and paddleboarding, among other water sports. Enjoy the breathtaking surroundings while taking part in exhilarating water sports adventures.

- **Beaches and Bays**: Along the cliffs are beautiful beaches and quiet bays that are great for swimming, sunbathing, and relaxing. The black volcanic sand on some of the adjacent beaches, such as Playa de los Guios, contrasts sharply with the soaring rocks in the distance.

- There are hiking and walking trails that provide panoramic views of the cliffs and the nearby shoreline if you want to explore on foot. These pathways offer a chance to get a close-up view of the area's natural beauty.

- **Restaurants & Cafés:** The town of Los Gigantes, which is at the bottom of the cliffs, has several eateries where you can have a delicious meal or a cool beverage while taking in the breath-blowing views.

A natural wonder that exemplifies the beauty and force of nature is the Los Gigantes Cliffs. The Los Gigantes Cliffs are a must-see attraction in Tenerife, whether you decide to explore the area on foot, take part in water sports, or enjoy them from a boat.

Anaga Rural Park

Anaga Rural Park, or Parque Rural de Anaga in Spanish, is a stunning natural area on the Canary Islands of Spain's Tenerife. What you need to know about this beautiful and varied natural park is as follows:

- Anaga Rural Park is renowned for its breathtaking landscapes, which are highlighted by lush green valleys, steep ravines, rocky cliffs, and dense forests. The rocky landscape of the park is the product of erosion and volcanic activity over millions of years.

- Anaga Rural Park has been recognized for its rich biodiversity and cultural history by being named a **UNESCO Biosphere Reserve**. It is a haven for numerous indigenous plant species and a haven for different bird species.

- **Nature and Hiking Trails:** The park provides a vast network of nature and hiking trails that wind through its varied topography. Visitors can use these paths to enjoy the splendour of the park on foot, with routes that cater to various levels of difficulty.

The paths take travellers to lookout sites, remote beaches, and charming towns.

- **Ancient Laurel Forest:** Laurisilva, also known as the ancient laurel forest, is only found in a few locations around the world, including Anaga Rural Park. With lofty trees, moss-covered rocks, and a distinct ambiance, this subtropical forest offers a lush and enchanting setting.

- **Taganana settlement**: Situated in a valley within the park, Taganana is a lovely settlement. Taganana provides a window into Tenerife's rustic and traditional way of life with its classic Canarian buildings and winding alleyways. It's a fantastic location for experiencing the local cuisine and culture.

- **Playa de Benijo**: Playa de Benijo is a gorgeous beach with black sand and striking rock formations that can be seen in Anaga Rural Park. It's a well-liked destination for surfers and outdoor enthusiasts looking for a remote and unspoiled coastal location.

- The iconic Teresitas Beach, the Anaga Mountains, and the Atlantic Ocean are all visible from the viewpoint known as Mirador de las Teresitas. It's a fantastic location for admiring the park's splendour and getting priceless pictures.

- Anaga Rural Park is a birdwatcher's dream come true. The Tenerife blue chaffinch and laurel pigeon, two indigenous bird species, both call the area home. If you want to see these feathery residents, bring your binoculars and explore the park's paths.

- **Picnic spots**: The park has set aside spots for picnics so guests can take their time eating in the great outdoors. With amenities like tables, benches, and BBQ grills, these places are perfect for picnics with family or friends.

Anaga Rural Park provides a serene and untainted natural setting that highlights Tenerife's distinct charm. A trip to Anaga Rural Park ensures a great experience in the midst of nature, whether you choose to hike along its trails, savour the ancient laurel forest, or take in the seaside vistas.

La Orotava

A lovely town called La Orotava may be found in Tenerife's north, one of Spain's Canary Islands. La Orotava, which is well-known for its extensive history, classic architecture, and lovely gardens, provides tourists with a magnificent window into the island's natural and cultural legacy. Here are some of La Orotava's highlights:

- **Old Town**: The historic core of La Orotava has been recognized as a Historic-Artistic Site and is home to classic Canarian architecture that has been expertly preserved. Take a stroll around the charming neighbourhoods' winding streets, which are surrounded with homes decorated with ornate facades, wooden balconies, and vibrant flowers.

- Casa de los Balcones is a classic Canarian home that exhibits the elaborate balconies (balcones) that the town is renowned for. It is a well-known landmark in La Orotava. Inside, visitors can browse a museum devoted to traditional crafts and shop for handicrafts and mementos made in the area.

- **Jardines del Marquesado de la Quinta Roja:** This magnificent park is a calm paradise full with rich foliage, fountains, and statues and is situated close to the town centre. It provides a tranquil setting for unwinding and taking in the wonders of nature.

- **Iglesia de la Concepción:** Located in La Orotava, the Church of the Conception is a magnificent example of Baroque architecture. It is a must-see for anybody interested in architecture because of its stunning exterior, opulent interior, and detailed woodwork.

- **Iberoamerican Crafts Museum of Tenerife:** This museum features a variety of traditional arts and crafts from Latin America and the Canary Islands. It sheds light on the shared cultural heritage of Tenerife and the Americas.

- **Plaza del Ayuntamiento**: With a lively ambiance and a central location, Plaza del Ayuntamiento is the town's principal square. Along with the Town Hall structure, it is flanked by eateries, stores, and cafes. A fantastic location to unwind and take in the atmosphere of the neighbourhood.

- The 16th-century mansion turned museum, Casa Lercaro, provides a window into La Orotava's past and present. The museum exhibits numerous facets of neighbourhood life, such as customary attire, furnishings, and artwork.

- The Mirador Humboldt overlook, which is located outside of La Orotava, provides stunning panoramic views of the city, the shore, and the surrounding areas. It's the ideal location to take in the area's natural splendour.

- **Fiestas & Traditions:** The lively and colourful festivals of La Orotava are well-known, such as the Corpus Christi celebrations in June, which are marked by magnificent flower carpets along the streets. The town's rich cultural heritage and traditions are on display during these celebrations.

- Gastronomy: Traditional Canarian cuisine is available in La Orotava. Try regional favourites including truchas de batata, bienmesabe, and (wrinkled potatoes) as well as mojo sauces.

A fascinating fusion of history, architecture, scenic beauty, and cultural traditions can be found in La Orotava. A trip to La Orotava is likely to captivate your senses and leave you with enduring memories of Tenerife's cultural legacy, whether you explore its historic centre, visit its museums, or simply meander through its picturesque alleyways.

Garachico And Icod de los Vinos

Two charming communities can be found on Tenerife's northwest coast in the Canary Islands of Spain: Garachico and Icod de los Vinos. Every town has a certain charm and charms of its own. What to expect when travelling to Garachico and Icod de los Vinos is as follows:

Garachico:

- **Historic Town Center**: Garachico is home to a historic town centre that has been preserved, complete with cobblestone streets, classic homes, and lovely squares. Admire the town's architectural wonders, such as the Church of Santa Ana and the Convent of San Francisco, while taking a leisurely stroll through it.

- **Natural Pools**: The El Caletón natural rock pools are one of the town's main draws. These pools, which were created by volcanic activity, provide a special location for swimming and taking in the Atlantic Ocean's pristine waters.

- **Castillo de San Miguel**: The village of San Miguel was previously shielded from pirate invasions by the San Miguel Castle, a mediaeval castle. From its battlements, it provides breathtaking views of the coastline and currently functions as a cultural hub.

- **El Drago Milenario**: El Drago Milenario is a 1,000-year-old dragon tree that can be found just outside of Garachico. This huge tree is regarded as being among the oldest and biggest of its kind on the entire planet. It is a must-see attraction and a representation of the community.

- **Plaza de la Libertad**: In the centre of Garachico, this attractive area is surrounded by vibrant buildings and is a lovely spot to sit and unwind. It's a centre for community activity and frequently holds markets and cultural events.

Icod of the Vinos

- **Ancient Dragon Tree**: The ancient Dragon Tree, also known as El Drago, is a famous feature of Icod de los Vinos. One of Tenerife's most recognizable symbols, this millennia-old tree is thought to be the oldest and largest of its kind in the entire globe. To observe this stunning natural wonder up close, travel to the Parque del Drago.

- **Historic District**: The town's historic district is distinguished by typical Canarian architecture and winding lanes lined with quaint homes. Discover the neighbourhood's stores and cafés as you stroll the streets and stop by the Church of San Marcos.

- The Cueva del Viento is one of the world's longest volcanic tubes, and it is situated not far from Icod de los Vinos. Learn about the island's volcanic past and explore the amazing subsurface lava formations on a guided tour.

- **Wine tasting:** The sweet Malvasia wine is especially well-known for being produced in Icod de los Vinos. Visit nearby wineries to indulge in wine tastings and discover the process of making wine.

- **Butterfly Garden:** The Mariposario del Drago en Icod de los Vinos is a special attraction with a tropical garden full of different types of butterflies. Visit the garden and take a leisurely stroll to see these beautiful creatures in their natural setting.

Icod de los Vinos and Garachico both offer a blend of historical, scenic, and cultural features. A visit to these villages offers a window into the genuine attractiveness of Tenerife's northwest coast, whether you explore the historic centres, take in the ancient dragon trees, or immerse yourself in local customs.

ITINERARIES AND TRAVEL PLANS

One Week in Tenerife

You'll have plenty of time to enjoy the variety of activities and experiences Tenerife has to offer if you only have a week to stay there. Here is a recommended schedule to help you make the most of your week:

Day 1: Get here and unwind

- When you go to Tenerife, find a place to stay and settle in.
- Take the day to unwind and get familiar with your surroundings.
- Visit a neighbouring beach, take a leisurely evening stroll, and explore the neighbourhood.

Explore Santa Cruz de Tenerife on Day 2

- Visit Santa Cruz de Tenerife, the island's capital, first thing in the morning.
- Visit the renowned Auditorio de Tenerife, stroll along the lively waterfront promenade, and explore the city's historic core.
- Visit institutions like the Museum of Fine Arts or Museo de la Naturaleza y el Hombre to learn about the local culture.
- Enjoy delectable Canarian cuisine at nearby eateries.

Day 3: National Park of Mount Teide

- Take a full-day excursion to the UNESCO World Heritage-listed Mount Teide National Park.
- For stunning views of the island and the surroundings, take a cable

car journey to the top of Mount Teide.
- Discover the distinctive volcanic landscapes, trek along beautiful paths, and be in awe of the natural treasures.
- Enjoy the park's magnificent skies and a sunset or a stargazing adventure.

Coastal exploration on Day 4

- Visit the charming communities of Garachico and Icod de los Vinos on Tenerife's western coast.
- Discover ancient dragon trees, stroll through historic districts, and take advantage of Garachico's natural rock ponds.
- In Icod de los Vinos, visit the renowned El Drago tree and stroll through the quaint alleys.
- Enjoy a leisurely evening by the sea, possibly watching the sunset

at a beach or coastal vantage point, to cap off the day.

Day 5: La Laguna and Anaga Rural Park

- Explore the lovely Anaga Rural Park by travelling to the island's northeast.
- Wander through the beautiful surroundings and historic laurel forests on a trek or nature walk.
- Visit Taganana to see the village's pastoral beauty and native culture.
- In the afternoon, go to La Laguna, a small town that is home to a university and also a UNESCO World Heritage site.
- Visit museums, explore the town's colonial architecture, and take in the vibrant ambiance of its squares and streets.

Day 6: Watersports and Beaches

- Spend the day exploring the stunning beaches of Tenerife and taking part in water sports.
- Visit well-known beaches like Playa de los Cristianos, Playa de las Teresitas, o Playa del Duque.
- Take part in aquatic activities like kayaking, surfing, snorkelling, or just unwinding on the fine sands.
- Enjoy fresh seafood and Canarian specialties while dining at the beachfront.

Masca and Los Gigantes on Day 7

- Take a day excursion to Masca, a quaint village in a lovely valley encircled by towering cliffs.
- Hike the well-known Masca Gorge, which is renowned for its amazing views and stunning natural beauty.

- After the hike, go to Los Gigantes to take in the breathtaking views of the sea-to-cliff cliffs.
- Visit the cliffs up close on a boat excursion, or unwind on one of the nearby beaches.
- Take in the local cuisine at a farewell meal to round off your day while thinking back on your week in Tenerife.

This itinerary allows you to enjoy the best of Tenerife in a week by combining cultural exploration, natural wonders, beach delights, and outdoor sports. Naturally, feel free to modify it.

Two Weeks in Tenerife

If you have two weeks to spend in Tenerife, you will have even more time to explore the island's attractions and become fully immersed in its rich culture and variety of landscapes. A proposed itinerary for a two-week visit is provided below:

Week 1:

Southern Coast & Beaches, Days 1-3

- Start your journey by touring Tenerife's well-known southern coast.
- Playa de las Américas or Playa de Los Cristianos both have beautiful beaches where you may unwind.
- Take part in water sports like diving, jet skiing, or snorkelling.
- Visit Siam Park, an action-packed water park with a variety of thrills and attractions.

- Take advantage of the area's exciting entertainment offerings and nightlife.

Days 4-5: The Area Around Mount Teide

- Give the beautiful Mount Teide and its surroundings two days of your time.
- Visit Mount Teide's Peak by cable car for sweeping views.
- Investigate the fascinating lava fields and volcanic landforms of Teide National Park.
- Take a hike on one of the park's many paths, such as the Roques de Garcia route.
- Visit Santiago del Teide and Vilaflor, two quaint cities.

Days 6–8: Northern Coast and Anaga Rural Park

- Visit the lovely Anaga Rural Park in the northeastern region of Tenerife.

- Hike through the historic laurel forests for a day while taking in the breathtaking views.
- Experience the charm of rural life by visiting the lovely village of Taganana.
- Discover the UNESCO World Heritage site of San Cristóbal de La Laguna, a historic city.
- Enjoy the beautiful coastal drives around the northern coast, including stops at breathtaking vistas and quaint towns.

Week 2:

La Orotava and Puerto de la Cruz on days 9 through 11

- The northern communities of La Orotava and Puerto de la Cruz should be explored for a few days.
- Admire the traditional architecture and gardens of La Orotava's historic centre.

- Discover the history of Canarian crafts in the Casa de los Balcones.
- Visit Puerto de la Cruz to unwind on its lovely beaches.
- Visit the well-known Lago Martiánez, a collection of César Manrique's seawater pools.
- Discover the numerous plant species in the Botanical Garden of Puerto de la Cruz.

Days 12 through 14: Tour the Western Coast

- Spend the last few days discovering Tenerife's western coast.
- Visit the natural rock pools in the quaint village of Garachico.
- Discover the quaint community of Icod de los Vinos and the historic Dragon Tree.
- Take a boat cruise to explore Los Gigantes' breathtaking cliffs up close and enjoy them.

- Go hiking in the renowned Masca Gorge and the Masca Valley.
- Explore the communities and rural countryside along the western coast for a day.

Make sure to enjoy the local food, try traditional Canarian delicacies, and sip some of the island's world-famous wines during your two-week stay. Remember to take some time to unwind and enjoy the serenity and beauty of Tenerife's breathtaking scenery.

Family-Friendly Itinerary

It's crucial to pick sites and activities that appeal to various age groups and interests if you're organising a family trip to Tenerife. A suggested family-friendly agenda for your visit is provided below:

Day 1: Get here and unwind

- Upon arrival, settle into your family-friendly lodging in Tenerife.
- Enjoy the day relaxing, taking in the surroundings, and getting to know the neighbourhood.

Beach day on day two

- Visit a family-friendly beach in Tenerife, such as Playa de las Teresitas o Playa de Los Cristianos.

- Play games at the beach, create sandcastles, and go swimming in the calm waters.
- For a relaxing family meal, bring a picnic lunch or check out some of the local restaurants along the beach.

Third day: Siam Park

- Visit Siam Park in Costa Adeje, one of the biggest water parks in Europe.
- Enjoy age-appropriate wave pools, exhilarating water slides, and relaxing rivers.
- Utilise the family-friendly amenities offered by the park, which include places specifically designed for children and areas where parents may unwind.

Day Four: Loro Park
- Visit the renowned animal park Loro Parque in Puerto de la Cruz for the day.

- Discover the wide variety of animal exhibitions, which feature penguins, dolphins, killer whales, parrots, and more.
- Watch amusing programs and instructive lectures all day long.
- Visit the botanical gardens in the park and take a picnic lunch in a beautiful outdoor environment.

Day 5: A Camel Ride and a Monkey Park

- Visit Monkey Park, a tiny zoo in Arona, where you can get up close and personal with several creatures, including lemurs, monkeys, and reptiles.
- Participate in feeding events and lectures to find out more about the animals.
- After that, take the family on a unique excursion with a camel ride in the southern region of the island.

Day 6: An underwater exploration and submarine safari

- In Puerto de Mogán, set off on a Submarine Safari excursion.
- Take a submarine ride into the Atlantic Ocean's depths to view marine life and the undersea environment.
- Enjoy the breathtaking views from the portholes while learning about marine life.
- Explore Puerto de Mogán's quaint streets and waterfront area after the submarine trip.

Day 7: Exploring a Rural Park

- Visit the Anaga Rural Park where you may enjoy stunning vistas while going on family-friendly treks through the park's lush woodlands.

- Learn about the park's flora, animals, and volcanic history as you explore the visitor centres.
- Enjoy a picnic in a natural setting at one of the authorised picnic spots.
- Take a leisurely drive down the charming seaside roads to cap off the day while admiring the breathtaking surroundings.

Day 8: Enjoy a free day to explore and unwind

- Take this day to leisurely explore and unwind.
- Choose from options like visiting local markets, going souvenir shopping, or just spending time as a family at the hotel or surrounding attractions.

Throughout your visit, be sure to sample regional specialties, enjoy family-friendly eating experiences, and try authentic Canarian food. Tenerife has a wide range of family-friendly activities and attractions to help everyone make lifelong memories.

Adventure Seeker's Itinerary

Here is a proposed itinerary for those seeking adventure in Tenerife who is looking for exhilarating encounters and heart-pounding activities:

Arrival and preparation on Day 1

- When you go to Tenerife, find a place to stay and settle in.
- Learn about adventurous activities and tour providers while becoming acquainted with the area.
- Rest, unwind, and get ready for the exciting days ahead for the day.

Paragliding on Day 2

- Start your voyage loaded with adventures by paragliding over Tenerife's breathtaking scenery.
- As you soar through the air, take in the stunning vistas of the island's shoreline.

- Pick from a variety of paragliding spots, including Taucho, Ifonche, or Adeje.

Third day: Scuba diving

- Scuba diving is a great way to discover Tenerife's underwater environment.
- Explore underwater tunnels and shipwrecks as well as colourful coral reefs and marine life.
- If you've never dived before, take a guided dive or sign up for a scuba diving school.

Off-Road Jeep Safari on Day 4

- Explore Tenerife's untamed landscapes by going on an off-road Jeep safari trip.
- Drive past breathtaking vistas, off-the-beaten-path paths, and mountain hikes.

- Take in the natural beauty of the island while experiencing the thrill of off-roading.

Canyoning on Day 5

- Take part in the heart-pounding sport of canyoning in Tenerife's breathtaking ravines.
- Rappel down cliff faces, pass through waterfalls, and jump into natural pools.
- Join a canyoning excursion conducted by knowledgeable guides who supply the required gear and direction.

Day 6: Either windsurfing or surfing

- The world-famous surf areas in Tenerife are the perfect place to catch some waves and enjoy windsurfing or surfing.

- There are options for every skill level, whether you're a novice or an expert surfer.
- Visit well-known surf spots like Playa de Martianez, Las Americas, or El Médano.

Day 7: Water sports and jet skiing

- Enjoy a day of jet skiing and water sports along the shore.
- Grab a jet ski and experience the exhilaration of speeding across the pristine waters.
- Try kiteboarding, wakeboarding, or other water activities like flyboarding.

Day 8: Masca Gorge hiking

- Start a strenuous hiking expedition in the renowned Masca Gorge.

- Trek through the difficult terrain while being encircled by stunning views and high cliffs.
- Enjoy the rush of overcoming the challenging descents and taking in the breathtaking scenery.

Mountain biking on Day 9

- On an exhilarating mountain biking excursion, explore the slopes and mountains of Tenerife.
- Take a guided mountain biking excursion or rent a bike to explore the island's various topographies.
- For an exhilarating ride, pick among cross-country routes, downhill courses, or volcanic scenery.

10th day: skydiving

- Try skydiving in Tenerife to take your adventure to new heights.

- Experience the rush of freefalling from a height of thousands of feet.
- As you drop beneath the parachute, take in the beautiful panoramic views of the island.

Rock climbing on Day 11

- On Tenerife's cliffs, test your limits by going rock climbing.
- Test your abilities on a variety of routes suitable for climbers of all experience levels.
- Explore the top climbing locations on the island by going on a guided climbing tour.

Day 12: Combination of canyoning and coasteering

- Combined with coasteering, canyoning makes for the perfect adventure day.
- Cross valleys, leap over cliffs into the ocean, and

Tenerife on a Budget

Don't worry if your trip to Tenerife is on a tight budget! The island has a wide range of reasonably priced choices for lodging, dining, and entertainment. Here is a recommended itinerary to help you maximise your inexpensive trip:

Arrival and exploration on Day 1

- When you reach Tenerife, find a hostel or cheap hotel to stay in and make yourself at home.
- To familiarise yourself with the region, take a stroll about it.
- Visit the free parks or beaches in the area for some outdoor leisure time.

Day Two: Uncharged Walking Tour

- Explore the key sights of Santa Cruz or Puerto de la Cruz by taking a free walking tour.

- Learn from skilled local guides all there is to know about Tenerife's history, culture, and architecture.
- After the tour, don't forget to give your guide a gratuity as a sign of appreciation.

Day 3: Examine the Beauty of Nature

- Without breaking your wallet, spend the day taking in Tenerife's stunning natural surroundings.
- Visit Playa de las Teresitas or Playa de Las Vistas, two breathtaking beaches renowned for their crystal-clear seas and golden sand.
- Visit natural parks like Parque Rural de Anaga or Parque Nacional del Teide, where admission is frequently free or inexpensive.

Visit local markets on day four.

- Investigate neighborhood markets like Mercado Municipal Nuestra Señora de Africa in Santa Cruz o Mercado Municipal de La Laguna.
- Learn about a range of locally produced foods, traditional snacks, and fresh produce.
- Get supplies for a picnic or inexpensive meals you can eat all day.

Day 5: A hike through the Teno Rural Park

- Utilise the stunning hiking trails in Tenerife's Teno Rural Park.
- Enjoy beautiful scenery, lush surroundings, and the serenity of nature.
- Utilise the park's free picnic spaces by bringing a lunch to share.

Sixth day: Free cultural activities

- Take advantage of the island's free cultural offerings.
- Visit museums like the Museo de la Naturaleza y el Hombre in Santa Cruz that provide free entry on particular days or at particular times.
- Attend free cultural performances, concerts, or events that are frequently held in public places or nearby venues.

Day 7: A beach day with water sports

- Enjoy the beach and some reasonably priced water sports for the day.
- Bring your beach gear and spend the day swimming, tanning, and unwinding.

- Try low-cost water sports like bodyboarding, snorkelling, or hiring a kayak or paddleboard.

Day 8: Examine regional food

- Visit small neighbourhood eateries, cafes, or street sellers to sample reasonably priced local cuisine.
- Try classic Canarian delicacies like almogrote (cheese spread) or papas arrugadas (wrinkled potatoes) with mojo sauce.
- During the lunch hour, look for "menu del da" options, which provide a fixed menu at a fair price.

Day 9: Explore Old Towns

- Discover the colonial architecture and quaint streets of the historic towns of La Orotava and La Laguna.

- Visit historical places and enjoy the architecture by taking a self-guided walking tour.
- Take advantage of free attractions like public gardens or overlooks while taking in the atmosphere of the town.

Day ten: Free outdoor pursuits

- Explore Tenerife's natural landscapes for free by hiking, bicycling, or picnicking.
- Find undiscovered beaches or secret locations for a relaxing and affordable day.
- Take advantage of the free or inexpensive amenities, such as public BBQ places or picnic areas, while taking in the lovely view.

Be sure to thoroughly consider your spending on your trip and hunt for bargains.

CONCLUSION

In conclusion, Tenerife provides visitors of all financial levels with a wide variety of experiences and attractions. Tenerife has something to offer, whether you're seeking opulent resorts, affordable lodging, adventurous pursuits, or cultural exploration.

You have been given a thorough picture of the island in this travel guide, including useful information, must-see sights, lodging alternatives, delectable cuisine, outdoor activities, shopping, nightlife, and more.

You may enjoy an unforgettable experience on this alluring island without going overboard if you carefully plan your trip and make use of the affordable options available. So pack your luggage, enjoy Tenerifc's beauty, and make lifelong travel memories.

Printed in Great Britain
by Amazon